My China Story: Crossing the Sea of Terror

By Chen Pokong

Translated by Stacy Mosher

Table of Contents

1. **Childhood: A Fate Foretold at the Age of Three** 2
   - The lingering trauma of the Cultural Revolution 3
   - A family shadowed by a burdensome background 3
   - My mother: An exquisite black box 4
   - My father: Awakened by the gunfire of Tiananmen Square 5
2. **Mao Dies, I am Reborn** 6
   - From middle-school waiting list to university student 7
   - Democratic awareness aroused by a book 8
3. **A Bold Petition to the Party General Secretary, Calling for Political Reform** 9
   - Encountering Jiang Zemin, then Mayor of Shanghai 9
   - A Letter to Hu Yaobang, then CCP General Secretary 10
   - A Grand Event to Welcome Fang Lizhi 11
4. **1986, Shanghai: An Earthshaking Student Movement, and My Birthday** 12
   - Tongji students forge ahead as a daring vanguard 12
   - A massive student protest on my birthday 13
   - Laying the foundation for the 1989 democracy movement 13
5. **Sowing the Seeds of Freedom, Launching the 1989 Democracy Movement** 14
   - Promoting democracy in money-mad Guangzhou 14
   - Establishing a cultural salon in preparation for the 1989 democracy movement 15
   - Public security agents infiltrate the democracy movement 15
   - Hu Yaobang's sudden death sparks protests nationwide 16
   - Producing more than thirty posters in one night 16
6. **Guangzhou: The Last Poem, the Last Resistance** 17
   - Gunfire in Beijing, tears in Guangzhou 17
   - The end of the nationwide democracy movement 19
7. **A Political Prisoner: Buried Alive, Worse Than Death** 20

- The ultimate bookworm falls into a trap 20
- Buried alive in the detention center 21
- Psychological warfare, interrogation and counter-interrogation 23
- A cage of iron and stone in the heart of the city 25
- Worse than death 26

8. My Lover, Hong: A Love Story in a Tragic Era 27
    - A heartless letter in anticipation of a long imprisonment 27
    - Hong panics over my disappearance 29
    - Caught between love and friendship in Shanghai 30
    - Bitter love, separated by time and space 30
    - Reunion beneath the high wall 31
    - A classic farewell 33

9. A Brave Letter to America about Blood-stained Flowers 35
    - An illegal crossing, and misfortune brought by a postage stamp 35
    - My Second Imprisonment: Becoming Spartacus 38
    - Rising to fame with one battle 39
    - A prison letter about blood-stained flowers 39

10. My Long Road to Exile, Far from Home 41
    - Advised to leave China, I go into exile 41
    - From student to principal: An American story 42
    - A worldwide following in the media and on the internet 44
    - Traversing the world but unable to enter my native land 45

1. Childhood: A Fate Foretold at the Age of Three

I grew up in the midst of terror. For a long time afterward, I suffered from phobia – experiencing sudden and unexplained anxiety and stress during peaceful everyday life. The doctors didn't refer to it as phobia, however, calling it "depression" instead. Only I knew it was phobia. I firmly believed that this was the more accurate term.

The lingering trauma of the Cultural Revolution

How did it all start? My father was brutally bound and taken away – not with ordinary rope, but with the kind that stonemasons use to lift rocks, as thick as a bamboo pole. Father was savagely beaten, not with ordinary wooden rods, but with the steel rods used by stonemasons. Father was pushed to the ground and publicly denounced. I'm told that sometimes what he knelt on was not an ordinary floor, but was strewn with glass shards. On these occasions, his blood flowed like water.

All of this is part of my earliest memories. Vague memories began when I was three. Binding, denouncing and brutally beating people were part of the scenario that Mao Zedong mapped out for his Great Cultural Revolution. Mao originally launched the Cultural Revolution because of his power struggle with President Liu Shaoqi, but it evolved into a class struggle that engulfed China as Mao vowed to purge the entire country of class enemies. Within the party, these class enemies were officials at various levels who followed Liu Shaoqi and his policy line; outside of the party, in the general population, they were intellectuals, households with the designation of landlord, rich peasant or capitalist, and families with connections to the old regime.

Terror accompanied me as I grew. In the middle of the night, I would often be awakened by low sobs. Needless to say, it was the muffled sound of my mother's weeping. Peering half asleep through the gauze mosquito net, I could vaguely make out a blood-soaked form curled on the floor – my father. Mother would be dabbing medicine on his wounds. In that small town, Mother was the only person formally trained in Western medicine, and she was renowned far and wide for her healing skills. Perhaps she had been fated to marry my father and constantly dress the wounds repeatedly inflicted on him.

Many times I was too scared to cry, and simply fell back into a deep sleep. In my dreams, a scene emerged over and over again, and lingered in my mind even after I awoke: A large wooden boat was capsized in a river that was also turned upside down, and I was in the boat with my head hanging down and my feet turned upward as the boat rocked back and forth, jostling violently as if trying to shake me off while I cried out in terror... This bizarre dream recurred throughout my childhood. I had no idea what that horrifying, topsy-turvy tableau was supposed to mean.

A family shadowed by a burdensome background

There weren't many scapegoats available in our small town, so my father, a high school teacher, was a focal target in every denunciation rally. The simple reason was that our family had the misfortune to fit the definition of several of Mao's "black categories": intellectuals, landlords and associates of the old regime. Father was a teacher and Mother was a doctor, which made them classic intellectuals; at the time that the Chinese Communist Party took power, my paternal grandfather was designated a landlord based on his possession of 11 *mu* (less than two acres) of hardscrabble farmland; and my father's second elder brother had graduated from the Whampoa Military Academy and had gone on to serve as an army commander under the Kuomintang. After fighting the Japanese in Shanxi, he returned triumphant to a hero's welcome in his home village. When the Communist forces occupied and liberated Sichuan in 1949, my uncle was commander of the Kuomintang defense forces in Santai County. Following negotiations with the Communists, he surrendered and brought a peaceful end to hostilities in that county. The Communists initially treated him like a VIP, but two years later, he was included among the quota of people arbitrarily suppressed in a "reexamination of land reform."

The actual background to this incident was that with the outbreak of the Korean War, the Communist government went back on its word for the sake of "stabilizing the rear areas," and suddenly rounded up and executed former Kuomintang civilian and military officers who had surrendered, gone over to the Communists, or been taken prisoners of war at the time of the Communist takeover. Reportedly, more than one million former KMT personnel were killed during this time. The gunfire of suppression ended my uncle's life, leaving a widow and three children, the youngest daughter still an infant.

When my paternal grandparents died soon after my uncle, the disreputable label "landlord family" descended onto my father's head, and he continued to suffer in their place throughout the years that followed. During every campaign or movement, he would be "plucked out" and subjected to brutal struggle and merciless attacks.

Several years after the Cultural Revolution began, I learned that my father had joined a political faction, the "rebel faction." The concept of rebel and conservative factions in rural towns was different from that in the major cities. In small towns, the rebel faction had no connection to the urban Red Guards, but simply opposed the local leadership. During the Cultural Revolution, local leaders changed as quickly as figures on a shadow lantern, and those who had once purged others found themselves subjected to the same treatment. Whether in schools or in commune party committees, the person taking charge was proclaimed the "genuine representative of Chairman Mao's proletarian revolutionary line." Once struck down, these same leaders were forced to "frankly confess" to having "opposed Chairman Mao's proletarian revolutionary line."

Although Father was labeled a member of the "rebel faction," he never took part in any armed struggle. Rather, he frequently wrote up big-character posters quoting Chairman Mao in wars of words with the "conservative faction." Quoting Chairman Mao was like wielding truth. Even so, Father was denounced and brutally beaten by others. Somehow he belonged to one of Mao's designated "black categories."

I'm so familiar with the Cultural Revolution that I can recite a stream of major slogans from that time. Members of the older generation are astonished; calculating by my age that I was only three when the Cultural Revolution began and only thirteen when it ended, they wonder how I know that history like the palm of my hand. They don't realize that my fate was decided at the age of three. The Cultural Revolution not only left me with indelible memories, but also had a profound and lasting effect on me; it left me traumatized and spurred my dreams of going far away. My subsequent discernment of the nature of autocracy and my desire for democracy are rooted in painful memories of the Cultural Revolution era.

My mother: An exquisite black box

In early 1972, the climax of the Cultural Revolution had just passed, resulting in denunciations of my father becoming slightly less frequent. Years of terror, sorrow and hardship had taken their toll on my mother, only thirty-four years old, and she was plagued with chronic illnesses borne of stress and overwork. Although a doctor, she could not heal herself. Father took Mother to Nanjing for medical treatment, but came back alone two months later carrying a black box exquisitely embroidered with the long-life symbols of cranes, pine and cypress trees and sika deer. In those years of material deprivation, when our clothing was stored in cardboard boxes, such an elegant box was an object of wonder to us children. It was in fact a cremation box. Our poor mother had been reduced to ashes.

Mother's abrupt passing turned our family upside down. She left behind four children, the eldest of whom, my sister, was thirteen, and the youngest, myself, only eight. From then on my father had to be our mother as well, gathering firewood, cooking our meals, and mending our clothing and shoes. My hard labor began at a tender age. Raising pigs, chickens, bees and rabbits, catching fish and snakes, gathering firewood... as we took full advantage of every means of livelihood, I labored among Sichuan's mountains and rivers year after year.

That was not the worst, however. The shadow of my family background shrouded me. "Landlord bastard!" That toxic curse spewing through the teeth of my head teacher thunders in my memory and has resounded throughout my life. My primary school head teacher was a hunchbacked middle-aged woman with a fiendish face, and her words were as cutting as knives. My sole advantage back then was being the top student in my class, and I was a natural leader, but at the least sign of ambition on my part, the head teacher would mobilize the entire class against me.

The head teacher should shout, "Isolate him!", and a new cycle of torment would begin. Bands of children followed me everywhere, shouting abuse: "Landlord!" "Landlord bastard!" Their insults were accompanied by barrages of spit balls, branches, mud balls and stones. All I could do was run for my life, often playing truant to avoid them. If I dared to fight back, I was reported to the head teacher, who scolded me shrewishly before the entire class: "You landlord bastard, how dare you attack the descendants of poor and lower-middle peasants!"

When Father learned of this, he was so angry that his mouth stretched into a tight line. He seemed to find the insults aimed at his son even more intolerable than his own persecution. Enraged, he hauled me to school to have things out with the head teacher: "You're saying my child is a landlord? How can an eight-year-old child be a landlord? He was born in the new society and has grown up under the Red Flag. How can he have exploited anyone, when even I have not? Not even Chairman Mao says that my child is a landlord!" The head teacher just sniffed and ignored him. During the Cultural Revolution, Father was persecuted, and throughout my years of elementary school I was persecuted along with him. It was a horrific childhood.

My father: Awakened by the gunfire of Tiananmen Square

Father taught high school music and art. During the last stage of the Cultural Revolution, I heard Father teach students to sing this song: "The Great Proletarian Cultural Revolution is good, is good, is good, is good!" I found the slogan-like lyrics boring. One day while Father was practicing this song, I couldn't bear it anymore, and summoned the courage to say, "What's so good about it! Look what it did to you!" Father gave me fierce look, his eyes filled with genuine reproach at words he considered nothing short of treasonous. He said nothing, however, apparently unable to come up with any convincing arguments.

Father had blind faith in Chairman Mao, and felt that everything was someone else's fault, while Chairman Mao was "sagacious." Father stubbornly persisted in this view even in the later stage of the Cultural Revolution and for years after it ended. As a result, as a teenager I often argued with my father until we were red in the face. Most of these arguments occurred during long trips on foot. Every few weeks, my father and I had to tramp over rugged hills and valleys from one small town to another far away. We covered dozens of kilometers in a day, sometimes to catch fish and other times to visit my elder sisters or brother, who were engaged in manual labor in other towns.

Father was finally awakened to reality by the gunfire of Tiananmen Square in 1989. I, his son, was sent to prison by the Communist Party for heeding the call of democracy. I was even stripped of my right to family visits. Many times my father set off with heavy bags from his home in Sichuan, wending his way to distant Guangzhou in hopes of catching a glimpse of his son, only to be mercilessly turned away by the Public Security Bureau. Father once stayed in my room in the unmarried quarters at Sun Yat-sen University while awaiting my release. Over the next month, he watched bees build a hive the size of a bowl under the dormitory window, but received no news of his son. I can't bear to imagine my father staggering tearfully away from dusty Guangzhou after this fruitless wait.

After a year in a dark, dreary jail, I suddenly received a letter from Hong, my girlfriend in Shanghai, which included a few heartbreaking sentences about my father. Hong wrote, "Uncle Chen wanted to come to Guangzhou and make lamps to support you... I talked him out of it." (Creating lamps for festivals was one of my father's special skills.) Heavens! My father had already gone through so much to raise me to adulthood, and with great difficulty had gotten me through graduate school. After working for two years I still hadn't begun repaying my filial obligation to him, and now my father, more than sixty years old, wanted to come to Guangzhou and toil to support me, a useless prisoner! Gripping the letter in my hands, for the first time during my detention I could not keep from sobbing.

After my release from prison, I found my father had changed. There was no more trace of his blind faith in Chairman Mao. Father now completely perceived the genuine nature of the Communist Party. He understood his son and understood democracy; not only did he not blame me in the slightest for my thinking and actions, but even expressed his unequivocal agreement and support.

2. Mao Dies, I am Reborn

I was the one fortunate child in my family thanks to Mao Zedong's death in 1976. The next year, China resumed its college admissions examination, and as the youngest in our family, I had the opportunity to take it. The death of a dictator brought rebirth to millions of people. As with the imperial examinations of ancient times, the college entrance exam gave Chinese young people an opportunity to stand out in the crowd.

From middle-school waiting list to university student

In my small town primary school, where I was humiliated by the head teacher, students were promoted to middle school through a recommendation system. That meant that the recommendation of school administrators, head teachers and classmates (who were obliged to obey the first two) determined who could advance to middle school. Through rounds of voting by raised hands, manipulated by the presence of the principal and head teacher, each student's name was written on the blackboard. Out of more than fifty students in my class, I was the only one not to be recommended for promotion to middle school, even though my academic performance had always been at the top of the class.

The terms "wait-listed" or "preparing for enrollment" were applied to students who had not been recommended for promotion. That summer, on the Honor Roll posted on the town noticeboard, a column headed by the term "wait-listed students" contained only one name – mine. At the sight of that humiliating notice, I prepared myself for the heartbreaking conclusion that I would not be allowed to continue my schooling.

A young man came to my rescue, however. This young man in his early twenties, who had just been assigned to the new middle school as a teacher of language and literature, and been designated a head teacher, had been a student of my father's. When he heard about my situation, he stepped resolutely forward, and resisting pressure, he insisted on taking me as his student as a form of repayment to my father. In his argument with school administrators, he said, "The boy is only twelve years old. If you don't let him go to school, what do you want him to do?" Other upstanding residents of the town who stood up for the disadvantaged also reasoned with the town leaders: "Why won't you let such a clever boy go to school?"

Mao Zedong died that year, and the college entrance exams resumed the next year. The school suddenly began emphasizing study, and as I entered my second year of middle school, my outstanding academic performance suddenly drew the applause of those around me. Placing first in my class, in the school and in our town, I was admitted to the key high school in the county seat and began sprinting toward college.

At the age of sixteen, I gained admission to Hunan University in Changsha – Mao's hometown. At that time, the percentage of students gaining admission to college was very low, and the few who were admitted to college were regarded as "favored by heaven." Ironically, just as I had been the only "wait-listed" student in primary school, I was the only student from my primary and middle school to gain admission to a university.

My dramatic transformation from a despised wait-listed student to widely envied and admired university student in the space of just four years was almost tragicomic. Yet upon receiving notice of my transformation to one of those "favored by heaven" by acceptance to Hunan University, I reacted by stamping my feet in anger and weeping inwardly. In middle school, I'd been forced to study sciences, for which I had neither interest nor aptitude, rather than being allowed to major in the humanities, which was my great interest and strength. This was related to the atmosphere of that era, when it was commonly said, "Excel in math, physics and chemistry and you can go anywhere." The liberal arts were ridiculed with a homophone that meant "plague subjects."

Gritting my teeth and grinding away at science subjects that I disliked, I didn't gain admission to one of China's best universities. Even worse, my assigned major in college was engineering, specifically designing roads and bridges. My four years of education in this profession were nonstop torture. As one of "fortune's favorites" in that era, I unwillingly accepted the share of "good fortune" that my older brother and sisters could only hope for.

Democratic awareness aroused by a book

I began reading *The Romance of the Three Kingdoms* when I was eight years old. As a child, I read almost every classical or modern novel available in China at the time. At Hunan University, all I thought about was going to the library and borrowing books I hadn't yet read. One book changed my life and triggered my earliest consciousness of democracy. The title of the book was *Stalin and the Soviet Communist Party*, by Abdurakhman Avtorkhanov, a fellow at the Soviet Academy of Social Sciences. This book, a record of Stalin's Great Purge, shocked me.

When I told other students about Stalin's Great Purge, their reaction was, "You've never lived in the Soviet Union, you didn't personally experience it, you didn't personally witness it, so how do you know it's true?" Without thinking, I answered, "Yes, all we can see is what's before us; all we can hear are the sounds around us; and our hands can only touch the things around us. But we have souls, and the soul can see even further than the eyes and hear more than the ear and reach deeper than the hand." Years later, the students who shook their heads in incomprehension finally understood and agreed with what I said.

Understanding Stalin's Great Purge made me realize that Mao's Cultural Revolution was the same kind of purge; both were the violent acts of dictators. Schemes and atrocities prevailed because of the evil of the totalitarian system. Only a democratic system under the supervision of the public could avoid this kind of man-made disaster. My burgeoning democratic consciousness gave rise to a political awakening. I was eighteen years old at the time.

In fact, I seemed to have an innate interest in politics, which also resulted from my constant reading and pondering. When I was in elementary school, one of the "faults" my head teacher criticized me for was my propensity for reading *Reference News*, an internal publication restricted to Communist Party cadres, which often reprinted foreign political news or historical anecdotes that ordinary newspapers were not allowed to publish.

By the time I went to Shanghai, my thinking had become far more mature and profound than that of other people my age. When I was twenty, I passed the exam for admission to Shanghai's Tongji University as a graduate student. This finally allowed me to abandon my detested major in engineering and shift to management, which greatly relieved my state of mind.

3. A Bold Petition to the Party General Secretary, Calling for Political Reform

Shanghai, China's top city, greatly broadened my horizons. At the graduate student phase, my course of study was relatively relaxed, giving me more time to explore China's future and seek out people with similar mindsets. By the mid-1980s, Chinese society was becoming more open, and the atmosphere on campus was vibrant. Within the Chinese Communist Party, reformists Hu Yaobang and Zhao Ziyang led the government, the elderly statesman Deng Xiaoping was China's gray eminence; and government control was relatively relaxed.

I often met up with other graduate students to discuss national affairs, criticizing the ills of the times and looking forward to democracy. By 1985, I had accumulated a large group of friends from various academic departments who shared my views. Because I was especially active, my fellow students elected me president of the Tongji University School of Management Graduate Student Union (elections were still allowed on campus at that time).

Encountering Jiang Zemin, then Mayor of Shanghai

In late autumn and early winter of 1985, I decided to launch a student movement in Shanghai to rally support for democratic reform. I used the pretext of commemorating the fiftieth anniversary of the 1935 December 9th Patriotic Movement, during which student protesters in Beijing had called on the government to resist Japanese aggression. In order to keep the arrangements secret, only I and around ten other close friends carried out the preparation work in strictest confidence. We spent several evenings writing out batches of leaflets calling for "Equality for all people, long live freedom," "Freedom, democracy, equality" and so on, until our hands were too cramped to stretch our fingers.

We packed our satchels with the leaflets, then took off in all directions on our bicycles to hand them out at other universities. Distributing the leaflets at other universities was a form of camouflage that I had thought of. With only a few of us handling multiple tasks, I took sole responsibility for nearby Fudan University. One Saturday afternoon, I rode my bicycle to the Fudan campus, the frigid wind of late autumn pouring down my collar. I spread our leaflets everywhere, on the Fudan lawn, seats in the lecture buildings, tables in the library…. On my way back to Tongji, I couldn't dispel my feeling of disconsolate loneliness. Why was I the only one engaged in this dangerous mission on the bustling Fudan campus?

Suddenly a typewritten note arrived from outside: The famous astrophysicist Fang Lizhi was giving a lecture at Zhejiang University. Professor Fang's debates on democracy were novel, daring and avant-garde, as well as easy to understand, incisive and inspiring to read.

My good friends and I promptly seized the opportunity to use wall newspapers and leafleting to promote Fang Lizhi's writings and speeches. Apart from Tongji University, we circulated these materials at all of Shanghai's major colleges and even outside of the city. In the name of the Tongji University Graduate Students' Union, we edited a volume entitled *Collected Speeches of Fang Lizhi and Yao Shuping* (Yao was another prominent scientist), printing 800 copies and distributing them to major universities. On the back cover of the collection I inscribed the words: Dissemination welcome for boundless merit." This covert publicity by my friends and me played a key role in spreading Fang Lizhi's fame throughout the country. I began a personal and respectful correspondence with Fang Lizhi in 1985.

Inevitably, however, a group of activists like us attracted the notice of university administrators and even of the State Security apparatus. This attention soon resulted in our being shadowed and monitored by plainclothes agents. One night, right after two friends and I pasted up a poster entitled "The Republic Needs This Kind of Scholar" (introducing Fang Lizhi's reportage) all around campus, administrators from the School of Management suddenly knocked on the doors of our dormitory rooms and sternly warned us not to put up any more posters. They had come under orders, and claiming to have our best interests at heart, they carried out "persuasion and education" work, admonishing us against causing further trouble.

The Shanghai authorities caught wind of our plans for a student demonstration on December 9 and hastily imposed an all-points crackdown. Jiang Zhemin, at that time mayor of Shanghai, came up with an off-the-cuff "masterstroke" by designating the week immediately before and after December 9th as "Traffic Safety Campaign Week." A massive inspection was carried out on transportation throughout the city, and a blanket ban was placed on any group activities on the streets.

With surveillance tight and rumors rife, I convened a meeting of the "student movement preparatory committee" to coolly analyze the situation. More than half of those present felt that the timing and conditions were not yet ripe to launch a student movement, so I proposed "quitting while we were ahead." After some discussion, the majority agreed with my suggestion, and we suspended our plans for the 1985 student movement.

A Letter to Hu Yaobang, then CCP General Secretary

Although we had put the student movement on hold, I suggested submitting a petition to the General Party Secretary of the Chinese Community Party (CCP), Hu Yaobang. I spent all night drafting it, and another friend copied it down. The gist of it was: Without political reform, there could be no economic reform; if political systemic reform was not carried out, in-depth economic systemic reform would be impossible; today's university students detested corruption and yearned for democracy; the student movement would help the government improve its work rather than "cause trouble."

The phrase "political systemic reform" is commonplace in China now, albeit in a distorted context. Back in 1985, those simple words never appeared in Chinese media or publications, and I was one of the first to propose them in our petition to Hu Yaobang. I never guessed that this basic tenet of democracy that I proposed as a young student would be regarded as a sign of "progress" in the Communist leadership when it finally issued from the lips of Premier Wen Jiabao more than twenty years later. (In 2012, Wen said, "Without successful political systemic reform, economic systemic reform cannot be carried out to its full extent.")[1]

We had prepared for a large-scale signature campaign for the petition, but many people who agreed with its content didn't dare sign it. The era was still dominated by a terror of speech crimes, and the horrors of the Cultural Revolution had inflicted lingering fears. At that time there was nothing unusual in someone being investigated and persecuted for petitioning the leadership or raising alternative views. Even the graduate student I'd assigned with the responsibility of delivering the petition to the post office removed his signature at the very last minute. As a result, only ten graduate students, with me at the top, signed the petition.

---

[1] Translator's note: See Chris Buckley, Nick Edwards, "China's Wen bets final year on reform push," Reuters, March 13, 2012, https://www.reuters.com/article/us-china-npc-wen/chinas-wen-bets-final-year-on-reform-push-idUSBRE82D07320120314.

Our uneasy wait brought positive results, however. In early summer 1986, Hu Yaobang sent two officials from the Propaganda Department of the CCP Central Committee (also known as the Central Propaganda Department) to Tongji University to engage in a dialogue with the ten of us who had signed the petition. Representing the signatories, I explaining our political views to the two officials: expanding democracy, extensively consulting public opinion and implementing political systemic reform. I spoke with passion, and the officials listened earnestly and took detailed notes. I thought to myself afterwards that Hu Yaobang was an unusually open-minded leader. Could it be that the Party's reformist faction would launch political reform in China?

A Grand Event to Welcome Fang Lizhi

In 1986, the atmosphere on campus was more invigorated than ever. Pluralistic thought trends galvanized the Idealism and longing of young students, and my friends and I often organized gatherings. After preparing the groundwork in spring and summer, by autumn we were ready to launch a Tongji University Cultural Movement sponsored jointly by the Graduate Student Union and the University Student Union. One of our objectives was to invite great cultural figures such as Fang Lizhi and Liu Binyan (a famous liberal writer) to give speeches.

On November 16, 1986, on behalf of the two student unions, I borrowed one of the school's Toyota sedans and a driver and went to the Shanghai Academy of Social Sciences to pick up Fang Lizhi and his wife, Li Shuxian, who had just returned to China after delivering a series of lectures overseas. On the drive back to Tongji, Fang said, "I'm not sure what topic you'd like me to speak on." After a moment's thought, I said, "How about this topic – democracy, reform and modernization." Fang immediately agreed: "Fine, that will be the topic!"

Democracy, reform and modernization had become the rallying cry for Chinese society in the 1980s. My classmates and I had scrambled around for days to arrange a grand reception for Fang and his wife. In the bulletin board at the center of the campus, I arranged a special section to welcome Fang Lizhi, welcoming Fang as the "national eagle." Every half hour, the campus radio station broadcasted a script I'd written notifying students that Fang would be coming to give a speech.

By the time I arrived with Fang and his wife, students were swarming inside and outside of the university's main auditorium. Tongji University, which specialized in architecture and construction, had designed China's largest unpillared auditorium, seating 5,000. On the day of Fang's arrival, the auditorium was packed solid, and even its corridors and surroundings were full of people who were unable to get inside, creating congestion all around the auditorium. Years later, in the United States, Fang told me that it was the grandest welcome he ever experienced in his life.

4. 1986, Shanghai: An Earthshaking Student Movement, and My Birthday

Visits by prominent intellectuals such as Fang Lizhi and Liu Binyan contributed to a whirlwind of new thinking on the Tongji campus. During this time, the campus seethed with excitement as Shanghai anticipated major changes.

Tongji students forge ahead as a daring vanguard

One month later, in December 1986, a democracy movement engulfed the entire country – the 1986 student movement. The student movement originated in Hefei, Anhui Province, the home of the University of Science and Technology of China, where Fang Lizhi was vice-president. The movement was sparked by elections to the people's congress. USTC students staged street protests against the "candidates" chosen by the university's administrators and promoted the election of Fang Lizhi and others. Fang was elected delegate to the people's congress with the highest number of votes.

When the news reached Shanghai, the first signs of action occurred at Jiaotong University. An American rock group performing at the Shanghai Sports Stadium invited members of the audience to dance on stage with them. When a student from Jiaotong University tried to go on stage, Party security personnel obstructed and beat him. The student returned to campus and described what had happened, sparking public indignation just as news of the student protests in Hefei arrived. Students at Jiaotong University decided to take to the streets off campus in protest against the government.

The Jiaotong University student protest was dramatically suspended, however, when Jiang Zhemin arrived on the campus for a "dialogue." An alumnus of Jiaotong University, Jiang had by then been promoted to Party secretary of Shanghai. At Tongji University, however, students poured off campus and forged ahead as the daring vanguard of protest. In Shanghai, Jiaotong was widely known as the fortress of democracy, while Tongji was the vanguard of the student movement.

I drafted a large number of publicity materials referred to as "big-character posters," which my friends copied and put up in the center of campus. This incited spontaneous gatherings of thousands of students from various departments, who poured out of the campus and took to the streets. Over the following week, an average of 8,000 Tongji students took part in protests every day, becoming the main force of the demonstrations. Tongji University's banner fluttered everywhere from the Bund and Nanjing Road to People's Square. One by one, Shanghai's universities joined the protest ranks led by Tongji students. Shouts of "Against corruption, down with profiteering," and "Democracy! Freedom! Equality!" resounded through the air.

A massive student protest on my birthday

The student movement reached its boiling point in the midst of frigid winter on December 19 and 20, 1986, with 70,000 university students holding street protests and an inestimable number of urban residents joining them or watching from the sidelines. The magnificent spectacle shook Shanghai. On December 20, a friend said to me, "Today is your birthday. How do you plan to celebrate?" At the time I was leading protesters in shouting slogans, but I paused for a minute and laughed, "Isn't this the best way? What could be more fun than celebrating with seventy thousand people!"

That day I marched in a sea of protesters through dozens of Shanghai's streets and alleys, passionately shouting slogans until I was hoarse. That was how I spent my unforgettable twenty-third birthday.

A group of students painted the words "Roll up autocracy!" on a reed bed mat, causing onlookers to jump up and down in delight. On behalf of the Student Movement Organization Committee, I changed a line in the Communist anthem "The Internationale" to "Democracy, freedom and equality / unites the human race." The eye-catching bed mat and altered version of "The Internationale" became symbols of the 1986 student movement.

Generally speaking, the 1986 student movement called itself organized, but it was very loose, with no centralized leadership. There were core organizers, but they were spread all around and each did things their own way. To a great extent, the student movement began and ended spontaneously. As final exams approached, the 1986 student movement that had engulfed more than a dozen major cities like a relay race, originating in Hefei and reaching a climax in Shanghai, finally ended in Beijing on New Year's Day, 1987.

Laying the foundation for the 1989 democracy movement

In mid-January 1987, as we were all busy with our final exams, we suddenly heard an announcement over the loudspeaker that Hu Yaobang had resigned as Party General Secretary. It turned out that Hu had been unlawfully dismissed by Party veterans led by Deng Xiaoping because of his sympathy for the students and inclination toward democracy. We later learned that the Communist authorities had dismissed Fang Lizhi, Liu Binyan, Wang Ruowang and other prominent intellectuals from their positions and had expelled them from the Party.

I immediately contacted my friends, and we pooled our funds to buy a big photo album, which we mailed to Fang Lizhi. On the title page, I painstakingly wrote lines from the poem "The Hard Road" by the great Tang poet Li Bai, but I changed the words from "A time will come to ride the wind and cleave the waves, and I will set my cloud-white sail across the raging sea" to "There will be ups and downs, but I will set my cloud-white sail across the raging sea." I used this poem to encourage Professor Fang with the thought that the democracy movement had not failed and would reach a new climax.

After Hu Yaobang was forced to step down, he became sidelined from the Party's circle of power, and with his aspirations frustrated, he sank into depression. On April 15, 1989, Hu suffered a heart attack and suddenly passed away. This is what triggered the 1989 democracy movement. Deng Xiaoping dispatched the army to suppress the movement, which ended with the massacre on June 4, 1989, now referred to as the June 4th incident or Tiananmen incident. In hindsight, the 1986 student movement in which I took a leading role actually laid the foundation for the 1989 democracy movement.

5. Sowing the Seeds of Freedom, Launching the 1989 Democracy Movement

The international community commonly uses the term the "Tiananmen incident" to refer to China's 1989 democracy movement and the violent crackdown by the Chinese government. Among China's citizens, including Chinese overseas, it is referred to as the "1989 democracy movement," or as the "June 4th incident" or "June 4th massacre." The Chinese government initially referred to the incident as a "counterrevolutionary rebellion," but subsequently played it down as "the political disturbance that occurred in 1989."

The hub of the 1989 democracy movement was China's capital, Beijing, and in particular the heart of Beijing, Tiananmen Square, where protests by a million students and residents drew the focus of the international media. Although the media took less notice of protests in other Chinese cities, they were also part of the 1989 democracy movement. In fact, the 1989 democracy movement occurred in more than 300 cities throughout China. Large numbers of people took to the streets all over China for nearly two months in late spring and early summer 1989, staging protests and demonstrations and submitting petitions demanding that the government obey the will of the people by launching democratic reform.

Promoting democracy in money-mad Guangzhou

After graduating from Tongji University in summer 1987, I was assigned a position as assistant professor at Sun Yat-sen University in Guangzhou. By "assigned" I mean that the government arranged the position, but in this case it conformed to my wishes. I had a romantic political aspiration of gaining experience in major cities such as Shanghai and Guangzhou, and then going to Beijing to round out my curriculum vitae. At the same time, I felt I had a mission yet to be completed: the democracy movement left unfinished in 1986.

Guangzhou, the capital of Guangdong Province, is referred to as China's "great southern gateway." The economic reforms of the Deng Xiaoping era began in Guangdong Province with the establishment of special economic zones in Shenzhen and Zhuhai, adjacent to Hong Kong and Macau, respectively. China's initial prosperity was buttressed by foreign capital entering Shenzhen through Hong Kong, and then passing through Guangzhou to China's hinterland.

"Guangzhou is all business, no politics." "Guangzhou resident only recognize money and nothing else." When I first arrived in Guangzhou and talked about democracy, people would smile derisively at me and make those comments with a cynical air. At first glance, Guangzhou was in fact predominantly commercial, with almost everyone engaged in business and finding ways to make money. Commercial Guangzhou, money-mad Guangzhou. Even so, I was unwilling to give up, and when I wasn't teaching, I went out on my own promoting democracy and making friends wherever I went.

"Don't talk to me about politics. I'm not interested," a student at Sun Yat-sen University name Chen Wei told me bluntly the first time we met. Even so, it didn't take long for this beautiful and impressive student to become an activist in the democracy movement. She eventually became Guangzhou's top student leader during the 1989 protests.

Establishing a cultural salon in preparation for the 1989 democracy movement

Relying on reason, passion and patience, I influenced more and more students and intellectuals like Chen Wei. By summer 1988, I had built up a circle of friends to begin to discuss what we needed to do. I suggested that 1989 was a significant year because it marked the fortieth anniversary of the People's Republic of China, the seventieth anniversary of the May Fourth Movement and the 200th anniversary of the French Revolution. We should organize demonstrations focused on those commemorative dates to demand political reform and promote China's democratization.

In this way, preparation work began for a democracy movement aimed at 1989. A weekly cultural salon was the first base we established. That was in January 1989 at Sun Yat-sen University, where we began openly holding campus gatherings to discuss democratic values and China's future, and I designated Chen Wei to run the salon. The students taking part in the discussions increased week by week, from just a handful at the beginning to eventually packing a lecture theater to standing-room-only capacity.

Once dismissed as a "cultural desert," Sun Yat-sen University began looking like an oasis. The atmosphere changed as the campus became more vibrant and democracy became a popular topic of everyday conversation. In this atmosphere, even if nothing major happened in Beijing, a new round of the student movement was certain to play out in Guangzhou.

Public security agents infiltrate the democracy movement

"So you're Chen Pokong!" A man surnamed Li shouted at Guangzhou's Sanyu Hotel one day in March 1989. I was meeting a journalist friend, who introduced me to this man, a secretary working for the Guangzhou provincial party committee. As we shook hands, Li said in a low voice, "An internal provincial party committee document says you're preparing to launch a student movement in Guangzhou."

My heart clenched as I immediately realized that public security agents had infiltrated the circle of friends I'd built up. Although we ran the cultural salon openly, preparations for the student movement were being carried out secretly among a much smaller group. It was impossible for me to immediately conclude who the agent was, but from then on, strange things began happening with increasing frequency. Whenever there was a meeting of the student movement preparatory committee, core members of the movement who had taken part in the meeting would quickly be called in for a chat by the leaders of their department (mid-ranking officials that the CCP placed in all of the universities) and would be warned not to "cause trouble." Clearly someone was informing on us.

I sought out reliable student movement leaders to discuss a method of dealing with the problem: Different people would attend different meetings without others being informed, and we'd see which group contained a leaker. This method worked well. We quickly discovered that a chemistry graduate student named Chen Yongchao was the informant. We later learned that he had joined the Ministry of State Security some time ago, and specialized in approaching activists on campus. His betrayal led to nearly all of the initial core members of the student movement being dealt with by the authorities.

Hu Yaobang's sudden death sparks protests nationwide

Finally a major incident occurred in Beijing. On April 15, 1989, Hu Yaobang, the former Party General Secretary who had been dismissed by Deng Xiaoping because of the 1986 student movement, suddenly died. As the news spread, unrest mounted throughout the country. At universities in Beijing and elsewhere in the country, public opinion roiled and commemorative activities fermented along with calls for the Deng Xiaoping government to restore Hu Yaobang's good name.

The greatest stir occurred in Beijing, where students from multiple universities quickly took action. Commemoration of Hu Yaobang quickly evolved into mass street protests criticizing official corruption and calling for democracy and freedom. In Guangzhou, the local government had set aside April 22 as a day for commemorating Hu Yaobang. Chen Wei and I and other student leaders appeared at Guangzhou's Haizhu Square to mourn Hu Yaobang and to publicly call for democratic reform. This was when Guangzhou's 1989 democracy movement formally began.

The movement reached its climax in May as people demonstrated in the streets every day in thousands or more than 100,000, and sometimes in the hundreds of thousands. Unrest roiled on both sides of the Pearl River, and banners fluttered beneath Baiyuan Mountain. Democracy activists in Guangdong and Hong Kong jointly held a massive street demonstration on May 23, 1989 that came to be known as the "great cross-border protest." On that day, more than 400,000 people marched through the streets of Guangzhou, and protesters swept through Guangzhou's major thoroughfares. Marching in this torrent, I joyfully exclaimed, "The people of Guangzhou aren't just creatures of commerce – they also long for democracy!"

My girlfriend, Hong, had been continuing her studies at Tongji University in Shanghai, but as students began boycotting classes across the country, she was able to come to Guangzhou. Reunited after a long separation, our romantic love merged with political fervor, and my life turned riotous with color and rich with meaning.

Producing more than thirty posters in one night

Limited by my status as a university instructor, I couldn't take to the streets as a student leader as I had in Shanghai. Apart from sometimes joining the street protests, my main work was writing all kinds of publicity materials and "big-character posters." Three major manifestos that I drafted, "An Open Letter to the People of Guangzhou," "An Open Letter to the Party and Government Cadres of Guangzhou" and "An Open Letter to the People's Army" were disseminated throughout the streets and lanes of Guangzhou.

Statues of Mao Zedong stood in the middle of college campuses all over China. The only exception was Sun Yat-sen University, where the statue in the middle of campus was that of modern China's first president, for whom the university was named. Alongside the bronze statue of Sun Yat-sen ran a long fence that served as a "wall newspaper" and was usually covered with notices about film showings, dance parties, lost items and school bulletins.

Once the student movement began, this wall newspaper became a discussion battlefield for the democracy movement. Piles of posters packed every inch of it, especially at the outset of the student movement, when it was common for more than thirty posters to appear in one night. A little-known secret was that nearly all of those thirty-odd posters came from my pen or were dictated by me and copied down by other students using brushes and ink. The handwriting on the various posters was different, and they were all signed differently, some by Intake Class of 1985 of the School of Management, Intake Class of 1987 of the Biology Department, Graduate Students of the Chinese Literature Department, Young Teachers of the Philosophy Department... The impression this gave of many people writing and putting up posters rapidly stoked the temperature of the democracy movement.

My dormitory room became known as the "CPK (Chen Pokong) Manuscript Center." After I was elected honorary chairman of the Independent Students' Organization, my dormitory room became the "second office" of the student movement. From it a steady stream of all kinds of publicity materials, speech transcripts and posters flowed to the frontlines of the democracy movement, into the hands of student leaders, and onto the wall newspaper at the center of the campus. My small room of less than twenty square meters was so packed with posters that visitors always stood gaping with surprise. This subsequently became the basis for the authorities arresting, prosecuting and jailing me for the "crime" of "counterrevolutionary propaganda and incitement."

6. Guangzhou: The Last Poem, the Last Resistance

Gunfire in Beijing, tears in Guangzhou

I was just falling asleep late at night on June 4, 1989, when student leaders Chen Wei and Yu Shiwen urgently knocked on the door of my room. With great distress they told me there had been a massacre in Beijing, that Deng Xiaoping had ordered the army to open fire, and that countless students and residents had been killed. Suddenly feeling as if a bullet had struck my heart, I lost consciousness. A short while later, I turned on the radio and tuned into a Hong Kong radio broadcast through a shortwave frequency. As news of the massacre was confirmed, tears streamed down my face.

Before this, most people, including me, believed that the authorities would not open fire, because the entire country was engulfed in the democracy movement. It was not only students and intellectuals but also ordinary citizens, workers and even establishment scholars and officials who had thrown themselves into the democracy movement. At its peak, even reporters from the Party mouthpiece, *People's Daily*, and cadres of organs under the CCP Central Committee had gone marching in the streets carrying banners supporting democracy.

I spent the night with brush in hand writing statements and posters, and had students copy them down and put them up in the middle of campus. Again there were more than thirty of them, including "Down with the reactionary government," "Resign from the Party and Youth League, take action urgently," "Condemn the massacre, bury dictatorship," and so on, appealing to students and professors to resist tyranny, and calling on anyone who had joined the Communist Party and Youth League to publicly declare that they had broken ranks with the ruling party.

Filled with grief and eyes streaming, I let my thoughts flow through my writing and wrote a poem that was also pasted on the wall newspaper. Entitled "Blood, Blood on Mother's Body," it went something like this:

Blood, blood on Mother's body

Did a nightmare awaken Mother
or did Mother shake the night awake?

Shouts pierce the ancient Imperial City
intense as the wind and wailing like rain.

Blood, blood on Mother's body

Gunfire rends the heavens
Tanks crush the dawn

The son cries for freedom
The mother cries for her son

Blood, blood on Mother's body

A 5,000-year-old mother
still bleeds in the gloom of night
not in bringing forth new life
but as a sacrifice for youth

Blood, blood on Mother's body

A mother whose tears fly like rain sees

her son's wing-borne soul among the clouds of chaos

Freedom is written on the sky

Freedom is not among humanity

Blood, blood on Mother's body

The end of the nationwide democracy movement

My previous certainty that the government would not open fire was based on faith in a bottom-line of humanity. At the same time, I was sure that if the government did open fire, it would be toppled as the entire populace launched a great rebellion and joined forces to overturn this morally bankrupt, cannibalistic regime.

But my twenty-five-year-old self was wrong. Deng Xiaoping, the dwarfish eighty-five-year old who controlled the military, steeled himself and brazenly deployed more than 200,000 PLA soldiers to surround Beijing and invade Tiananmen Square, using tanks and machine guns to wash the ground with the blood of unarmed students and citizens. I was also wrong in that the majority of China's people did not revolt, but cravenly abandoned the struggle. Apart from the streets of Beijing, where residents and students maintained a courageous life-and-death resistance for one day and one night, everyone else scattered like birds and beasts.

There are two classical Chinese sayings: "Shoot the bird who sticks his neck out first," and "Kill the chicken to warn the monkeys." Deng Xiaoping shrewdly calculated that if he could suppress the democracy movement in Beijing, the democracy movements in other parts of China would also die out, and in fact, after the June 4th Massacre, the democracy movements elsewhere in China rapidly subsided. Protests in Guangzhou continued for three days with the blocking of bridges and roads, but the number of participants declined drastically over time.

The students voluntarily disbanded. Some went into hiding, some returned to their hometowns and others began preparing for their final exams. Witnessing this situation filled me with sorrow and despondency. My ears still reverberated with the cries of just a few days ago, when students marching in the streets thunderously shouted, "Sun Yat-sen U! Sun Yat-sen U! Nurtured by the people, we will die for the people!" It seemed that the two-month democracy movement was nothing but a romantic ballad. Now those who had joined together had scattered, and everything had returned to the same oppressive reality as before.

7. A Political Prisoner: Buried Alive, Worse Than Death

The ultimate bookworm falls into a trap

I and student leaders of the local democracy movement found ourselves in a dangerous situation, isolated and cut off from help. Beijing issued its "Arrest Warrant List," and Guangdong issued a "Public Notice List." The difference in the titles indicated their different meanings: "Warrants" implied that people were to be pursued, captured and arrested, while "public notice" required those on the list to report to public security organs to "talk" and "confess their problems." Compared with Beijing, the Guangdong authorities were more inclined to deal moderately with democracy movement leaders. Guangdong's provincial governor, Ye Xuanping, was the son of Communist veteran Ye Jianying, who belonged to the politically moderate faction. My name and Chen Wei's topped the list of "four main democracy movement leaders" in the public notice.

At the age of twenty-five, I was the ultimate bookworm, impractical and naive. I didn't feel I'd done anything wrong, so instead of going on the run, I headed off to the Public Security Bureau to have a "talk" with the authorities. In my mind was engraved the old Chinese saying: "A good man is defined by his acts." In the meantime, I continued tutoring students for the final exams. Sometimes a student would ask me, "Teacher Chen, why don't you run away? I hear that Wuerkaixi [one of the student leaders in Beijing] has already fled to Hong Kong!" Half-jokingly I would reply, "The success or failure of our motherland is my personal success or failure. I'm willing to advance or retreat along with the motherland."

My "talks" with the Guangzhou Public Security Bureau continued for a month. The PSB officials tried to "educate me" and get me to "confess" or change my thinking. Given our different standpoints, these talks usually turned into rounds of debate that devolved into fierce arguments. PSB officials mopped their sweating brows with handkerchiefs to hide the frustration and anger on their faces.

As I headed off to another appointment with the PSB on the afternoon of August 2, 1989, Hong saw me off by giving me an apple and gently saying, "An apple [*pingguo*] brings peace [*ping'an*]. Come home soon!" Who would have known that I would never return after leaving that day?

The weather was scorching hot under the blazing southern sun, and I felt like I was being cooked in a steamer. As I passed through the western gate of Sun Yat-sen University, someone called my name. Just as I was automatically responding, four unknown middle-aged men came at me from different directions, blocking the sunlight with their tall, brawny forms. Half coaxing and half shoving, they maneuvered me into a sedan with curtained windows. Alternatively nervous and cool-headed, I was taken to an unknown location.

The four men were plainclothes State Security agents, and on that day I lost my freedom after being formally arrested and sent to a detention center. As I entered prison for the first time in my life, I suddenly regretted my bookish naivety and idealism. Why hadn't I run? My talks with the PSB had been used against me, and I had walked straight into a trap.

Chen Wei and other student leaders were also arrested one by one. It turned out that the central government in Beijing had put direct pressure on the Guangdong authorities, criticizing them for being "hard on one side and soft on the other" (pushing hard for economic reform, but soft on politics), and ordering them to follow Beijing's example by immediately arresting and prosecuting the leaders of the Guangdong democracy movement. After that, Deng Xiaoping removed Ye Xuanping from Guangzhou and "kicked him upstairs" to Beijing, where he was given the purely ceremonial position of vice-chairman of the Chinese People's Political Consultative Conference.

Buried alive in the detention center

The gate of Hell opened before me, and I entered, calming my inner terror as best I could. Its appearance and conditions gave me the immediate impression that I had descended into a Hell on Earth.

It was a large compound, in the center of which rubbish was piled into a small mountain. Grey buildings stood along four walls topped with barbed wire. Before I had time to take full measure of the environment, someone pointed a camera at me, and my eyes clamped shut against a blinding flash. It was a photo for a press release or an official file, and I hastily pushed my undershirt beneath my belt to present a tidier appearance. I calmly followed the direction of their waving hands to show that I was neither fearful nor defeated.

I was taken into one of the gray buildings. In a room marked "Escort Room," I was surrounded by a group of people, some in uniform and some in plain clothes. They carried out a body search, making an inventory of everything I had with me and saying they would have to put those things in safekeeping for me.

After the body search, someone took me to a room on the second floor marked "Inquest Room." There several uniformed PSB officers confirmed my name and date of birth and then ordered me to sign my name on a sheet of paper. One of them, who looked like a senior officer, told me in a consoling tone of voice that this was a temporary measure referred to as "Custody and Examination." Naive as I was back then, I didn't know that custody and examination meant indefinite detention. I preferred to believe the consoling tone of the official and think this was just another talk in a different location.

When I glimpsed the words stenciled on a chair, "Guangzhou Municipal Public Security Bureau Detention Center No. 1," I learned the name of the compound and building I was in. Even then I didn't immediately connect the term "detention center" with prison. Vaguely remembering the phrase from the old civil war novel *Red Crag*, I considered it an obsolete term.

I asked, "Where am I?" The others replied by looking at each other. I asked, "When will I go home today?", and they looked at each other again. The senior officer blandly told me, "I'm afraid you can't go home for the time being." My heart sank. I thought of Hong and wondered whether she knew and what she would do. I immediately became very upset.

Someone took me to the third floor. The metal bannister on the stairway was corroded with age. A fantasy suddenly flashed through my brain: One day I would race out of here like a puff of smoke. For a moment I longed for the abilities of the Monkey King, Sun Wukong. "Now that you're here, don't get any crazy ideas," a low voice muttered behind me just at that moment, as if to dispel my notion.

I had two new escorts, one rather old and the other quite young. Both were detention center corrections officers who worked in this building. The corridor was only wide enough for two or three people to pass through it abreast. Occasional narrow iron doors were set into the solid walls.

Metal clanged as an iron door opened next to me, and the older corrections officer motioned me inside. With a loud rumble accompanied by a muffled sound, the heavy iron door closed behind me, the rumbling continuing to resound deafeningly in my mind forever after.

My small room, if it could be called that, had a ray of light, and raising my head to look at it, I saw a window at the top of the wall, covered by crisscrossing thick metal rods. I had only a few seconds to ponder this when a noise came from behind me, and a pair of rheumy gray eyeballs – those of the older corrections officer – appeared in a pane of frosted glass about the size of my palm. This was quickly followed by a hand motion indicating that I was to stand to the left. Another iron door rumbled to my left, narrower than the one before. As I hesitated, I again saw the eyeballs and hand motion appear one after another in the small window, and having no choice, I stepped through a doorway barely wide enough for one person.

There was another rumbling sound as the narrow iron door closed behind me. It turned out that this was an iron gate that slid between upper and lower rollers and was controlled from the corridor outside my cell. In the days that followed, I understood that the outside room was called the airing cell and the inner room was called the holding cell. Even so, my mind was still blank, and I had no concept of a prison cell.

My eyes had not yet adjusted from the glaring city streets to the tenebrous detention center, and everything seemed to be in shadow. Fate had banished me to the darkness. As my eyes adjusted, the pitch blackness turned to dusk. Someone called, "Here, this way!" I dimly saw a board bed raised slightly above the ground, and on it sat three bare-chested men. At this point I once again became conscious of the summer heat. I later learned that these three men were my cellmates.

I always shared my holding cell with three or four other prisoners, but I was the only political prisoner; the others had been jailed for economic crimes, and all were cadres from the public security apparatus who were being held on corruption and bribery charges. Although they were prisoners, they were also responsible for keeping an eye on me, imposing a dual imprisonment.

I'd anticipated ending up here sooner or later; there was no avoiding the calamity of imprisonment. My rebellious nature was bound to become intolerable to this system. It had taken me twenty-five years to end up here. A detention center was just another name for a prison, and slow as I was to catch on, I eventually understood its full significance.

The peak of terror was not on the first day, when I entered prison, but when I awoke on the morning of the second day, shooting up in bed at the urgent ringing of a bell. Where was I? I looked around, panic-stricken. The space was so narrow, and the walls on all sides were so high that when I put on my glasses I saw that eye-level hit only the midpoint of the solid cement wall across from me.

The wall was covered with words. Glancing upward, I vaguely made out the word "surveillance" on the top line. I quickly turned my head, as if that would help me avoid further misfortune. I wouldn't look because I didn't belong here, my heart insisted. It wasn't until the day that I left this narrow space to be transferred to another detention center that I saw that the word wasn't "surveillance" but rather "regulations," and that the dense writing below it listed the detailed rules and regulations of the detention center.

I felt as if my life had been abruptly interrupted, and that I had been cut off from all contact with ordinary life. I couldn't participate in anything outside, or care about it, but only look on helplessly. It was like the soul of the dead suddenly knowing everything about life, but being unable to do anything but talk to the living in dreams, like the warning in the poem "Regrets of Impermanence" from *The Dream of the Red Chamber*: "With wide-open eyes abandon all things."

I suddenly noticed my three cellmates listening carefully, even though I couldn't hear anything; all was silence in the corridor outside our cell. But after a few minutes there was a banging sound, and a hatch the size of a dog door opened on the wall beside us. "Time to eat!" came the runner's shout, and four dented aluminum mess tins were shoved inside.

Low-grade rice, wilted vegetables and two pieces of filthy-looking fatty pork. That made up the two daily meals in the detention center. Irregular pig bristles carelessly left on the meat showed that the cooks knew they didn't need to make any effort for the people they served. The first time I ate this prison food, I had to choke it down, especially the pieces of dirty, fatty pork. They seemed design to disgust, and almost made me vomit.

"Eat up! Who knows how long you'll be shut up in here!" a rail-thin prisoner advised me. Once head of a PSB vice squad, he had been locked up for more than three years without his case being closed. I took his words very seriously. "You're right, I have to survive! I have to get used to all of this," I thought to myself. I chewed, pressing my lips and eyes shut against the disgusting taste, like a child swallowing bitter medicine in one gulp.

Psychological warfare, interrogation and counter-interrogation

"5342!" "5342!", the prison guard called after the cell door opened. The second time was an impatient shout. Here I had become a number: 5342.

During the first month, I was occasionally taken to the second floor to be interrogated. A fat middle-aged man the size of a buffalo sat behind the rostrum. He was the inquest officer in charge of my case, nicknamed "Judge." To his left there usually sat a secretary, responsible for recording the proceedings. Sometimes the secretary was a man, other times a woman. When the secretary was a woman, I noticed them occasionally pass notes back and forth with shifty looks on their faces; the notes clearly had nothing to do with the case.

In my mind I gave the fat man another nickname, "Big Black Bear." Nodding complacently, Big Black Bear announced, "There are three ways to confess: The first is dumping it all out at once; the second is turning on the faucet; the third is squeezing it out like toothpaste, little by little. You can think it over and decide which way you'll choose." Then he said sonorously, "Our party's policy is to treat frankness with leniency and resistance with severity."

Yet, in the cell I heard private conversations between prisoners who had been public security cadres, who all said, "Frankness and leniency keeps you in prison, resistance and severity gets you home for the Spring Festival." In other words, the Communist Party tricked you into confessing, not to be lenient, but rather to frame you.

A thumping sound next door was followed by hair-raising screams. The interrogating officer and the secretary paused for a moment and exchanged glances, then looked at me as if considering whether they should let me hear those kinds of sounds. The advantage was that hearing it might make me more compliant; the disadvantage was that it might make me look for loopholes in their legal system...

"Close the door," Big Black Bear said softly to the secretary, an indecisive look in his eyes. A moment later, Big Black Bear said to me, "You're lucky. Ten or twenty years ago, political prisoners like you would also have been beaten half to death." What he was implying was that the person being tortured next door was a criminal, while I was being treated differently as a political prisoner.

I worked out that the Chinese government was under pressure because of international concern over the Tiananmen incident, and that although it had arrested leaders of the democracy movement, there were misgivings about employing torture.

The inquest, referred to as "being brought before the court," involved interrogation and questioning, but instinctively gave rise to counter-interrogation. Through Big Black Bear's hints, I could infer how much my adversaries already knew and what they didn't know; I could also guess, regarding those outside, who had revealed or concealed what information. This was psychological warfare, staking the intelligence of the interrogator against the person being interrogated. Big Black Bear was not as smart as he thought.

Instead, Big Black Bear's questioning allowed me to understand the inclinations of the authorities. At that time, all of Chinese society outside of the prisons, and especially academia, was engaged in a campaign arranged by the Chinese government for "everyone to pass the test." This meant that everyone, regardless of whether or not they had participated in the democracy movement, had to write a report confessing what they had done, or what they had seen those around them doing during the democracy movement. If they had participated in street protests, they were required to criticize their own actions and admit their error to the Party. Otherwise, if they were Party or Youth League members, they would be expelled; if they had jobs, they would be dismissed; and if they were students who were about to graduate, they would not be assigned jobs, or only the worst kind.

Many people throughout the country, at colleges, in government organs and in state-owned enterprises, folded under the threats of the authorities and complied with their orders, writing confessions and acknowledging their errors, as well as informing against others. Just two months earlier they had enthusiastically participated in the democracy movement, impassioned and burning with righteous indignation! And now... The farcical process of "passing the test" fully exposed the condition of Chinese society and the character of the Chinese people.

Reports exposed me as an instigator and ringleader who directed the entire Guangzhou democracy movement, which may have been true in terms of how it all started. At the age of twenty-five, I was the "backstage manipulator" of the Guangzhou democracy movement and the Party's top enemy in Guangzhou. That is what the authorities had determined, and I was obliged to take responsibility.

A cage of iron and stone in the heart of the city

An almost hermetically sealed cage of iron and stone was located in the throbbing heart of the city. Humanity streamed outside the walls that held those inside in captivity. Outside, people bustled around earning a living, unconscious and uncaring of what occurred within the walls.

This cage of iron and stone was the No. 1 Detention Center of the Guangzhou Municipal Public Security Bureau, also known as the Huanghua Detention Center for its location on Huanghua Street, a minor thoroughfare deep within the city's core. I had been thrust into this cage, and once the heavy iron door closed behind me with its muffled rumbling sound, I was utterly cut off from the rest of the world.

If this large, gray building could be called a cage, each cell within it was also a small cage. Both the large and small cages were sealed off by compressed reinforced concrete. It was nothing like depicted in movies, where it is possible to peer inside and outside of the prison. Here I couldn't even see the corridor outside my cell.

This sealed-off stone and iron cage measured around two meters wide and three meters long, for a total of six to seven square meters. The ceiling crowned four extremely tall, thick and heavy walls made of reinforced concrete. For all its poverty, China has never stinted on brick, stone and iron rods to buttress its prison walls. The "tofu dregs construction" that causes buildings all over China to collapse with the merest shove would never be found in prisons.

High up on one wall, beyond the reach of a human hand, was what could be called a window, crisscrossed with thick iron rods and covered on its exterior with iron netting. This only source of fresh air was thus filtered through iron, as were the sun's rays that spread through the cell. A light on the ceiling was kept on twenty-four hours a day, but even in the broadest daylight the cell remained in murky darkness, as a prison cell is meant to be.

The Chinese term for the small cage can be directly translated as "warehouse." It must be acknowledged that this is an accurate designation. Like a warehouse, a prison cell stores goods, in this case living human beings. During the inquest stage, prior to sentencing, living human beings are stored temporarily in this place, even if "temporarily" means many years or an indefinite duration.

Over time, even my opportunities to be "brought before the court" disappeared. I became no more than a commodity stored in the dark, damp, muggy warehouse, day after day and month after month. I sensed that this "indefinite period of imprisonment" resulted from the authorities having trouble deciding how to deal with a democracy movement leader.

In fact, this was even more frightening than being sentenced, because at least with a sentence I'd know how long my imprisonment would last; until then, being held indefinitely was inexpressibly terrifying. Many times I found it impossible to extricate myself from the deep delusion that things had always been this way, and would remain so for eternity. This system that claimed to want to "reform" me ultimately served only one purpose, which was to intensify my innate phobia and make me thoroughly rebel against it.

My concept of time was subverted; what I had once measured in hours, minutes and seconds I now measured in days, months and years. Who said "Time is more precious than gold"? Clearly, "Time is harder to spend than gold." Facing the abyss of time, I consoled my fellow prisoners by saying, "In fact, we spend only half of our time in prison." When they looked at me in confusion, I continued, "The time we're sleeping doesn't count, because we're immersed in our dreams. In our dreams, we're free and not in prison." The other prisoners' eyes lit up, comforted by these words.

Worse than death

I subconsciously raised my left arm toward the trickle of sunlight that reached one corner of the airing cell. A sore on the back of my hand was healing more slowly than it should have. I'd gotten it by accidently bumping my hand against the edge of a water vat several months ago. I wondered if I had contracted diabetes, for no reason other than that I'd heard that the wounds of diabetics take longer to heal.

During my drawn-out incarceration, I observed unusual physiological changes. At some point my hair, once soft, became as coarse as withered grass and finally stood straight up like needles. I didn't dare continue using soap, because it seemed to dry my hair out even more.

My once oily skin likewise became as dry and coarse as snake skin. My skin became fragile, bruising and bleeding with the slightest bump. Scraping myself on a wall or water vat left a black-and-blue mark that took a long time to fade. When the weather was hot, a kind of granular skin ulcer that the prisoners called scabies would spread all over, as if my body was rotting. Water became a corrosive agent, just one drop intensifying my athlete's foot and making it unbearably itchy. I could find nothing to scrape it with; the prison authorities confiscated all hard items on the pretext of preventing suicide or escape attempts.

Eventually I understood that my hair had become coarse and my skin fragile because of prolonged lack of sunlight and fresh air. Although there was an airing cell, the partition that separated it from our holding cell was seldom opened, and never for more than half an hour at a time. Furthermore, the so-called airing room was just another cell with a barred window at the top of the wall. The heavy foot tread of armed soldiers was constantly audible outside the window, like the sound of German Nazi soldiers marching in their combat boots in the movies.

This cage of reinforced concrete represented the height of human ingenuity. Animals, for instance tigers, don't imprison each other, but humans completely seal each other off from all outside contact. Is that what it means to be an "advanced animal"? Intelligence has turned humans into the darkest type of animal. I suddenly recalled the old saying, "Even the most vicious tiger doesn't devour its young." But humans are evil enough to eat other humans, and not just metaphorically; during China's Great Famine in the 1960s, there were outbreaks of cannibalism, and families even exchanged their children to eat.

In the martial arts novel *The Return of the Condor Heroes*, by the Hong Kong author Louis Cha, I read a phrase: "the tomb of the living dead." This expression was a perfect metaphor for my prison cell. Truly, it was a tomb, differentiated from a normal tomb only by the fact that living people were buried in it.

I was alive, but buried, buried alive. I never guessed that I would spend two and a half years buried in this cage of iron and stone, this tomb of the living dead! It was experiencing death, or a taste of it. It was not death, but worse than death; a near-death experience. Even the physical changes in me were like what happens in death. All that remained alive was my soul.

Like the spirit of a dead man, I initially remained attached to the mortal world and concerned about everything in it. Gradually I faced reality and accustomed myself to occupying an alternative space. Human beings are unusual creatures with an inconceivable ability to adapt to any environment, no matter how dangerous or brutal. Gradually, a person cuts all ties with the outside world, as if never associated with it in the first place. Especially when my cellmates and I discussed our individual cases, and guessed what kind of sentences they would draw, the frame of reference was no longer the outside world but rather the community of prisoners within the cell. Accepting one's fate is a human instinct.

8. My Lover, Hong: A Love Story in a Tragic Era

Almost without realizing it, I experienced summer, autumn, winter and spring in prison. I had entered prison in summer, and before I knew it, summer had arrived again, the summer of 1990. A banging sound suddenly came from outside the opening in the wall, and a letter addressed to me was stuffed inside. This was a surprise. Political prisoners are monitored much more strictly than those jailed for criminal offenses, and I seldom received letters.

A heartless letter in anticipation of a long imprisonment

The letter had been opened, according to usual practice, for examination by prison officials. I was both happy and anxious to see it was from Hong. After scattered communications during the first stage of my imprisonment, we had become untethered from each other. Apart from locking me up, the authorities cut off all my ties with the outside world and categorically prohibited family visits. Ordinary prisoners had no trouble getting letters and visits, but in the eyes of the Communist Party, political prisoners were more dangerous than ordinary criminals.

Hong wrote in her letter, "...I've graduated from college. The government assigned me to the Chongqing Municipal Personnel Bureau. But I decided to go to Guangzhou and find a job with a foreign enterprise and wait for your release...

My heart shrank. Hong was from Chongqing and had previously told me that after graduation she had no intention of returning there. The authorities had clearly ordered her to go there against her will as a disguised form of punishment. Furthermore, she hadn't been assigned a specific job, but had just been handed over to the Chongqing Municipal Personnel Bureau, which implied a malicious intention to toy with her. Graduates of high-ranking universities such as Tongji normally enjoyed preferential treatment.

The next part was about my father, and it shocked me deeply. Hong wrote, "Uncle Chen wanted to come to Guangzhou and make lamps to support you... I talked him out of it." I suddenly cried out in sorrow, disregarding the other prisoners around me. It was the first time I'd done this in the detention center. I was full of sadness and longing for Hong, for my father and for my ruined life.

Tears streamed down my face and dripped onto Hong's closing inscription, "Your little boat, Hong." That signature distressed me even more. In one of the countless love poems I'd written for Hong, I'd called her "my little boat." Those days of love and romance were gone forever!

Indefinite detention, a dark road with no end in sight. The inquest official had even threatened me, "You'll sit there long enough to wear through the floor!" Young, beautiful, intelligent Hong had already given up so much for me. I couldn't allow her to continue to suffer on my behalf.

Several times I'd dreamed of Hong killing herself because she couldn't stand the government's harassment and society's scorn, and of myself kneeling and sobbing before her grave, the green grass spreading in all directions until I disappeared in it. "No! No!" After waking up, I would shout this to myself and cry out to God, "I'll bear all of the world's torment and pain rather than allow Hong to suffer. I don't want anything to happen to her! God, please help me! Let Hong escape her hardship! Let her live! As long as she's alive and safe, I'll spend the rest of my life in prison without regret!"

Steeling myself in my pain, I wrote a letter to Hong: "... Fate has obstructed our road to happiness, and the foundation of our happiness had been destroyed. Yet half remains, and that is you, your youth, your beauty, your freedom...

"... At this time, I have only one request: Leave me, take your youth and beauty and run, fly, far from me. Don't think of me ever again. As long as you can be happy, my heart will be happy; your happiness is my happiness. Because I love you; I will love you forever...

"Please don't worry about me, truly, I can face anything and carry on. You, only you, are the source of my weakness, the only and ultimate source. Without you, I have nothing left to worry about. I will be able to endure whatever comes..."

In order to renounce my self-interest and ensure her staunch resolve, I ended the letter with forceful language:

"You have never let me down, and I believe that you will also not let me down in the future. The best way for you to not let me down now is to leave me. Run, fly far away. Really, leave me! Run, fly far away!"

The cramped cell had no corner where I could grieve to my heart's content. The other prisoners sat beside me. After I finished writing, I bowed my head on my knees as if sleeping and allowed my tears to flow like rain. I wanted to snap my pen in pieces to show that everything was over, but the plastic ballpoint pen simply would not break. Finally I bent it and tossed it into the garbage can.

The next day, I handed my letter to the older corrections officer and repeatedly begged him to send it out, no matter what. "I will never bother you again after this!"

Hong panics over my disappearance

It was only after my release from prison that I learned what Hong had gone through back then. On the day that I left and didn't come back, Hong panicked and ran all over trying to find out what had happened to me. At one point she went to Sun Yat-sen University's security office (the security apparatus that the authorities had set up within the university), but they had no information to offer. She went to the Guangzhou Public Security Bureau, but they told her I wasn't there. Hong protested, declaring that she would sit there and not leave until she saw me. A public security official then pretended to comfort her, saying that I was staying in a decent place and was being treated well, but that I couldn't go home for the time being and that she shouldn't worry.

That afternoon, after being shoved into my prison cell, I suddenly realized that Hong didn't know where I'd gone. Disregarding all else, I pounded on the iron door. As my pounding became more intense, corrections officers rushed over and opened the slot in the door. I angrily yelled, "You have to see my girlfriend and let her know where I am." After a moment, I was taken again to the second floor, where a PSB officer said they couldn't let Hong see me for the time being, but that I could write a short note, which they would take to her.

At the time I was arrested, I was distinctly aware of worrying not about myself but rather about Hong, about whether she could endure what had happened and how she was managing. At the thought of her pretty, delicate face, tears poured from my eyes and dripped onto my arm. The PSB officers were next to me, and I absolutely couldn't let them see my weak side, so I hid my tears by pretending to wipe my glasses. I picked up a pen and wrote, "... I love you now more than ever before; at this moment, you are my only concern..."

I searched for words to comfort Hong. "...Every matter is a process; every process eventually ends..." At the end of the letter, I suggested that she return to Shanghai as soon as possible and prepare for the new school year.

Having no alternative, Hong returned to Shanghai and continued her studies at Tongji University. State security and public security officers constantly disturbed her by demanding that she "explain and expose" my problems. The other students could study and live normally, but Hong had to bear the dual pressures of being separated from her lover and interrogated by the authorities. She was subjected to endless harassment.

Later I also learned that Hong came to Guangzhou several times in hopes of seeing me, but like my father, her requests were mercilessly refused by the Guangdong authorities. They only allowed Hong to send clothing, which they then passed on to me while lying, "The leader of the Sun Yat-sen University economics department brought these for you." The Guangdong authorities not only prevented Hong from seeing me, but also took the opportunity to make her life difficult and to blackmail and humiliate her in hopes of getting evidence from her that they could use against me.

The painful image of Hong, a delicate, beautiful young woman, dragging a heavy suitcase all by herself between Shanghai, Guangzhou and Chongqing plagued my memory for the rest of my life.

Caught between love and friendship in Shanghai

Hong and I fell in love on the eve of the 1986 student movement in Shanghai. Pretty, vivacious, graceful Hong was the object of admiration for many male students, to the point where she caused a rift between me and my good friend Jie. Jie had pursued Hong without success, his taciturn nature apparently incompatible with the lively, cheerful Hong, and as a result, he became dejected.

At that time, I'd been through several love affairs and had no plans to court anyone else. Yet, Hong and I fell in love without intending to. We had a group of friends in common who often got together to talk and go around sight-seeing. A group of male graduate students and a group of female undergrads seemed to form a perfect team, and we not only had a lot of fun together, but inevitably paired off in romantic relationships.

Perhaps it was Hong's beauty and vitality that gradually attracted me; perhaps it was my sense of humor and love of telling jokes that unintentionally attracted Hong. When Hong and I suddenly fell hopelessly in love, Jie fell into a painful despair over his heartbreak. The love between Hong and me was therefore initially accompanied by deep and painful feelings of guilt toward Jie. When it comes to making choices between love and friendship, emotions hold sway and complicate things.

I tried to preserve my friendship with Jie by giving up Hong for a time. That was easier said than done, however, and whenever we encountered each other, or even merely exchanged a glance, the vines of love grew from the fields of our hearts and climbed upward intertwined. The more we exercised restraint, the more vibrant our love became. The vine couldn't be kept from growing, and became too deeply rooted and vigorous to destroy.

After the 1986 student movement, our love emerged from the haze, and my friendship with Jie and other good friends was also gradually restored. But the good times couldn't last, and after a passionate half year, I graduated and was sent to Guangzhou to work, while Hong still had three years left of the studies that kept her far away from me. At that time, China's transportation consisted mainly of trains, and traveling from Shanghai to Guangzhou took nearly two days and a night. With one of us working and the other still in school, we faced hardship in meeting as well as in parting.

Bitter love, separated by time and space

Separation by time and space could not obstruct our love, but it caused us infinite distress. From then on our lives were inundated with longing, waiting and sorrowful partings. To this day I can't bear to look at lovers kissing each other goodbye at a train station or airport. It makes me think of my partings with Hong back then, when tears soaked our clothing. That sadness and despair at being parted pains my heart to this day.

I regretted going to Guangzhou to work, but the circumstances in China at that time made it impossible for me to transfer to Shanghai, and Hong could also not transfer her studies to Guangzhou. All attempts to change jobs or schools ended in failure.

In the middle of semesters, while students were reviewing for their mid-term exams, I would secretly leave Guangzhou and spend a short time with Hong in Shanghai. Winter breaks also presented us with happy reunions. Yet, it seemed that we met only to be parted, and we paid for our short-term happiness with long separation. Shanghai, Guangzhou, Chengdu, Chongqing, Mianyang, all were sprinkled with the tears of our parting. Our passionate words and solemn pledges of love were no match for the ruthlessness of time and space. As the train began to move, we looked at each other tearfully, and at that moment, no one seemed to exist in this world but us, a pitiful pair of lovers!

One time, as we were saying goodbye at the Shanghai train station, I suddenly said to Hong, "How pathetic we are! I'm worse off than your watch, which can grip your wrist; I'm worse off than your satchel, which can accompany you; I'm worse off than this umbrella, which can protect you from the sun and rain..." We broke down in tears before I could finish.

Our profound anguish made our love even deeper. After two years of this torment, in May 1989, with students boycotting classes at all of China's universities, Hong came to Guangzhou, and we could finally be together in freedom and happiness.

Our excitement and passion continued for more than two months, until I was arrested and imprisoned. Hong besieged the authorities, but could not find out what happened to me, much less see me, even for a moment.

You see, this love survived conflicts of friendship and separation in time and space, becoming even more intense, tenacious and deep-seated. Even God became jealous and flew into a rage, making the country break out in stormy tumult – the 1989 democracy movement, the June 4th massacre, and in this way finally managed to separate Hong and me completely on either side of a high stone wall.

Reunion beneath the high wall

Going back to summer 1990, after I sent the letter ending our relationship, I received no more messages from Hong. The loss of all news of her was like dropping a stone in the ocean. Half a year later, in February 1991, I was suddenly indicted, and during my court trial in March I was sentenced to three years in prison for "counterrevolutionary propaganda and incitement." This sentence was comparable to those imposed on democracy movement leaders in Beijing and took account of international pressure. In Guangzhou, a three-year sentence was the heaviest handed down to democracy activists; other student leaders were detained or sentenced for one to two years.

Among them, student leader Yi Danxuan was sentenced to two years, and Chen Wei was detained for a year and a half. Another student leader incarcerated in the cell next to mine, Yu Shiwen, was released after enduring a year and a half at the detention center. Just before he left, he yelled out my name, told me he was leaving, and urged me to take care of myself. I yelled back for him to take care. Bouncing off the ceiling and filtered through the thick walls, our voices came out soft but distinct. After that I was silent, listening to the iron door clanging shut and the disorderly sound of departing footsteps.

After sentencing, I was moved to the No. 2 Detention Center in Guangzhou's northwestern suburb of Tan'gang. Ordinary criminals are banished to labor reform farms after sentencing, and at least there they can enjoy some sunlight and fresh air. I could only envy them as I remained shut away in the tomb of reinforced concrete, without even access to an airing cell. At least the judgment allowed me to know that I had to serve only another year and a half. Silently I breathed a sigh of relief.

I spent another year sealed away in the dark, humid and sultry cell, my hair as dry as straw and my skin festering day by day. My vision also began to suffer, so I occasionally did handstands against the wall, having heard that this could help preserve eyesight.

I spent an estimated two and a half years of my three-year prison term buried alive in the tomb. After I protested again, the authorities made special arrangements for me in the last half year: During the daytime I could labor in a garden on the detention center grounds, but at night I'd be locked up in the cell again. My meals also substantially improved.

As the completion of my sentence neared, the authorities intensified their persuasion work on me, referred to as "education and rescue." Two public security officers came to see me every one or two weeks, apparently the only time they thought of this not insubstantial "cargo" stored in the detention center. They urged me as if with my best interests at heart, using the mildest possible tone of voice to impress on me the great principle of "stability above all else."

They even went to see Hong at the foreign company in Guangzhou where she worked, attempting to enlist her in the government's persuasion work. As a result, Hong became the only person I was allowed to see throughout my three years in prison. At that time, I had only three months left before being released. The garden of the No. 2 Detention Center where I labored during the day had an old-fashioned pavilion surrounded with water on four sides, connected to the rest of the garden by a small wooden bridge. That evening, Hong was brought to the pavilion to see me. After nearly three years of bitter separation, we were finally reunited beneath the prison's high walls!

The Hong who appeared before me was as beautiful as ever, but unexpectedly, she also felt strange to me, and I believe I also felt strange to her. This unexpected feeling of estrangement separated us like the ocean and chasm of time, and at first we didn't know what to say to each other. A cool wind blew through the evening air, and the chirping of frogs rang from the pond. We talked about inconsequential things, and I even stammered, as if long imprisonment had deprived me of my ability to speak.

Officials from the public security bureau and detention center sat beside us to monitor our meeting, making for an awkward scene. The stipulated half-hour passed very quickly, and at my request, the officials extended the meeting by another half hour. Finally the public security official declared that time was up. Hong stood to take her leave, and we smiled forcedly at each other. With throbbing heart I watched for a long time as her lovely figure, clothes fluttering in the breeze, disappeared into the night.

The public security officials believed that Hong and I would reunite after I left prison, which would encourage my "law-abiding" and "stable" behavior, but my intuition was more accurate. Hong, with her smiling face, bland expression and excessive courtesy, had experienced a fundamental change. I should no longer complicate or disturb her life.

A classic farewell

Three months later I was released from prison. I had no choice but to contact Hong, because she was holding some important documents for me. That day was the last time I saw her.

It was the evening of August 10, 1992, at Guangzhou's Jiangnan Hotel on the bank of the Pearl River. Freezing air conditioning blasted through the lobby to keep the intense summer heat at bay. When Hong appeared, I felt self-conscious about my basic and unfashionable clothing.

"Chinese or Western food?" Hong asked, turning to me as we made our way to the second floor. I was dumbstruck for a moment. Having been cut off from the world for three years, I didn't know what had changed, not to mention how to choose a meal. "How about Chinese," I said off the top of my head. A group of fashionable young men and women, boisterous with food and drink, staggered laughing down the stairs. As they brushed past, they suddenly became silent and looked attentively at Hong while measuring me up. As always, Hong drew the admiring gaze of passers-by in public places, with a very high "head-turn rate." At that moment I couldn't help but feel grossly inadequate.

The restaurant on the second floor was designed to look like a pavilion. My impression is of tables, chairs, floor and ceiling made of solid teak, as glossy as lacquer and beautiful as new. Once we sat down I finally had a chance to closely observe Hong; I hadn't been able to see her clearly that evening three months ago in the detention center garden.

She wore a pale yellow jacket, a full pink skirt cinched with a dark red belt and black high heels. Her silky shoulder-length hair was drawn into a bouncy bundle behind her neck, with stray hairs floating alongside her face. A polka-dotted hairclip was fastened along one side of her hairline. All of the colors were bright and eye-catching in a way that I later realized had become fashionable that year.

Hong herself remained unchanged. Apart from dressing even more beautifully, not a hair of her outward appearance had changed over the past three years, and she was still a ravishing beauty. It was only that the sense of unfamiliarity from our meeting at the detention center still came between us, as shown by our exaggerated courtesy toward each other.

A casual glance at the menu made me jump a little. Twenty-five *yuan* for one cold appetizer? Hong was paying for the meal that night, and it seemed to me that she spent money like water. After dinner, we went elsewhere for a cup of coffee and continued talking, our words interspersed with silence.

Sitting across from each other, Hong and I casually told each other all we needed to know about the past few years. Hong had brought my packet of identity documents, including my school transcripts and diplomas, and said, "I wish you a promising future!" I said, "I wish you splendid prospects." Several men sitting a few tables away kept sweeping us with their gazes, and I worked out that they were plainclothes agents. As long as I remained in China, I would never be free of this shadowing and surveillance, especially when I met others.

It was a classic farewell in a classic ambience. From the second floor where we sat, we could lean over the railing and scan the lobby below, where brilliantly dressed men and women came and went, brushing past each other. A band performed along the carved railing. Was that "Auld Lang Syne" they were playing? I knew the tune, called "Everlasting Friendship" in Chinese, from the movie *Waterloo Bridge*.

With love's silent retreat, feelings and love had become unmentionable topics, and we instinctively avoided them. By tacit agreement, Hong and I confined our conversation to random social topics, like ordinary friends.

We had met at six o'clock. At ten o'clock, Hong said, "I guess that's it." I nodded and said, "Yes, that's about it." We were referring to the length of our meeting. She said she had to make a phone call. Not far away was a wooden structure shaped like a telephone kiosk. She picked up the receiver of the pay phone inside.

I sat alone, swirling my coffee cup, deep in thought. With little effort I caught a few of Hong's words coming out of the telephone kiosk: "....the thirteenth.... flight.... Shanghai." My intuition was correct. There was already someone else in Hong's life. I could also sense that Hong had resigned from her job in Guangzhou. And in fact, after parting from me, Hong left Guangzhou for good.

We descended the shiny teak circular staircase, Hong elegant and poised as she walked with delicate steps, her skirt swaying. Compared with the pure beauty of the past, this new Hong looked more regal. I walked two steps behind her and watched the undulation of her lovely hair, and especially the white back of her neck, adorned with a fine gold necklace. It made me remember a small wish she had, when we were first in love, for a fine gold necklace to wear. As a poor student, I didn't have the money to buy it for her, but after I graduated and began working at Sun Yat-sen University, I finally satisfied her wish. The moment the sparkling gold necklace was fastened around her neck, Hong's eyes flashed with joy.

Looking at the elegant beauty in front of me, our many pledges of undying love flashed through my brain, and I couldn't keep my heart from clenching. Was this how we would part? Is this how she would leave? Was this how that surging passion would end? I looked calm on the surface, but countless thoughts and scenes from the past mingled in my brain.

Too soon we reached the lobby. We passed through the hotel's revolving doors, where taxis were lined up at the entrance to take people away. Hong turned and asked me, "Should you go first, or should I?" I automatically replied, "You first, of course." Before climbing into the taxi, Hong turned and waved at me, a smile blossoming on her face. I wanted to smile, but could only manage to wave back robotically. I could sense that my expression was rigidly solemn.

I jumped into the next taxi, and the driver asked, "Where to?" Seeing Hong's taxi heading toward the north end of the Haizhu Bridge, I pointed the driver in the opposite direction: "Go to Jiangnan Avenue South."

My once beloved Hong disappeared into the darkness among the mass of humanity. I never heard from her again. On the day we parted, I didn't anticipate how deep and great the wound would be. I continued to cherish her memory and long for her in the years that followed. I couldn't dispel the image of her that filled my dreams, and often awoke with tears in my eyes. I've always been such a sentimental person.

I went from depressed to haggard to prematurely aged, my appearance changing so drastically in the course of one year that I hardly recognized myself in the mirror. One day I suddenly tossed away the mirror and shouted to myself, "I have to leave China!"

Dusty Guangzhou and its streams of gaudy young people were only misty images to me now. Had life lost all its meaning for me? After Hong left, my life went into freefall down a bottomless black hole. This hollow life and hollow mindset would become irreversible if I continued this way. Until I ended up in Hell. Until I left China.

Eventually, after my second spell in prison, I published a collection of poems entitled *Rumors* (Guangdong People's Publishing). Most were love poems I'd written for Hong, or were about our love affair. A title like *Rumors* was unlikely to attract the notice of the authorities, and using an unrecognizable pen name, I evaded the censorship of cultural officials. Publishing this poetry collection was meant to commemorate that love, and at my request, a photo of Hong was printed on the back cover of the book. It was almost the only photo I had of Hong, taken years before at Sanhaowu Lake at Tongji University.

9. A Brave Letter to America about Blood-stained Flowers

My three years of imprisonment ended, I returned to society full of hope, but those hopes were quickly dashed. I was still splattered with the hot blood of 1989, but all I saw around me was stuporous extravagance and masses of people living in a dream world. I found it impossible to merge into this era of rampant debauchery, or to accustom myself to a society reeking which the stench of money.

"The courtesan, ignorant of the pain of perished empires, continued to sing across the river." All I could think of was these lines from Tang poet Du Mu's poem when friends dragged me to a dancehall. My mail was inspected, my telephone was tapped, I was shadowed wherever I went, and every month I had to have a chat with the public security bureau. That was life for me in China in the 1990s after I left prison.

An illegal crossing, and misfortune brought by a postage stamp

My second imprisonment was virtually predestined. The year that I attained my freedom, I went back to Sichuan to visit family. One day in Chengdu, I was waiting for someone on Nine Holes Bridge when a fortune-teller walked over, repeatedly calling, "Sir! Sir!" and insisting on telling my fortune. I flippantly said, "If you can tell me my past, I'll let you tell my future." He spoke just two sentences, and they astounded me: "One of your parents died prematurely." After scrutinizing my face and my palm, he went on, "You've been in prison." I sized up the fortune-teller, who was unusually short and bizarrely dressed in a long, gray topcoat that brushed his feet, and decided to let him tell my future. "If you're not careful, you'll go to prison again," he tossed out.

And that's what happened. After returning to Guangzhou, I worked for a foreign company while continuing to promote democratic thinking by delivering magazines and books to friends in my spare time. As a result, the PSB subpoenaed me repeatedly. "Don't give up without a fight." After being called in to the police station yet again, I decided to learn from past experience and prepared to flee China at a moment's notice.

Just at that time, former Guangzhou student movement leaders Yu Shiwen and Chen Wei, now married, came to Guangzhou to see me. Nothing could have been more gratifying than this reunion of old friends. We seemed to never run out of things to talk about, and conversed deep into the night. Analyzing the situation inside and outside of China, and my personal difficulties, I told them of my plan to cross illegally into Hong Kong and escape to freedom, and suggested that they go with me. After some hesitation, they finally accepted my suggestion and said they might as well give it a try.

We set off separately, and after doubling back and around the downtown area and finally losing my plainclothes surveillance, I shoved my way onto a long-distance public bus headed for the seafront. I met up with Yu Shiwen and Chen Wei in a border town as previously arranged.

We learned of a remote fishing port where captains of fishing trawlers or speedboats accepted fees to take people to Hong Kong almost every night. Most of the people who entered Hong Kong illegally this way were going there to work. We boarded one of the power speedboats, called "big flyers" because they flew over the water. Sometimes we could hear bullets whizzing past the boat. Finally the "big flyer" evaded the mainland police boat, and around midnight it pulled up to the Hong Kong coast.

Yet, having escaped the tiger, we encountered a wolf. It was our bad luck to fall into the captain's trap. As the "big flyer" neared a beach, the captain whispered to us, "We're here! We're here! Get going!" In the depths of night, the three of us scrambled onto a rocky beach while the speedboat turned tail and sped off with the other passengers. Later we realized that the pilot had used us as bait to distract the Hong Kong police, and after dropping us off he had carried the rest of his passengers, which included his close friends and/or relatives, to another beach so they could look for underground jobs in Hong Kong.

We, the unwitting bait, immediately fell into the hands of the Hong Kong police. Upon clambering to the top of a steep cliff, we were greeted by the blinding beams of flashlights. "Don't move!" someone shouted as a group of policemen surrounded us.

The policemen took us to an Immigration Department detention center located on hill called San Uk Lang. Fluent in Cantonese, I explained our backgrounds and situation to the Hong Kong authorities in hopes that they would give us political asylum. But a few days later, we were repatriated to the mainland with a group of other illegal immigrants. By the time I discovered that the Hong Kong police had confiscated my identity card and other important items, the black van full of illegal immigrants had already crossed the border into Guangdong.

Only four years after the Tiananmen crackdown, things had changed, and former democracy movement leaders had become persona non-grata, even in pre-handover Hong Kong.

Upon arriving at a custody center, we and the other failed immigrants paid our fines and left. That night there was a drenching rainstorm, and I waded through knee-deep water searching for shelter. Concerned about Yu Shiwen and Chen Wei, who had been taken to a different custody center, I hurriedly asked friends to help them. Fortunately Yu and Chen were released soon afterwards.

Our first escape attempt went unnoticed by the Communist authorities. But I was determined to return to Hong Kong and at least recover my main identity documents, including my ID card, my previous court judgment and a valuable postage stamp commemorating June 4th. I remember that on the night we reached San Uk Lang, a policeman examining our personal belongings yelled, "Look, it's that postage stamp!" Several other officials and policemen crowded around and pushed each other away to look at it.

In 1992, the Chinese government had issued a set of postage stamps commemorating the twenty-fifth Olympic Games. One of the stamps triggered a major uproar. The stamp showed several runners, and the numbers on the shirts of the first three athletes read 64, 9 and 17, but with 17 looking like the Chinese character for 8. Read backward, the numbers came out as 8964, and the Chinese term for "reading backwards," *daonian*, sounds the same as the term for "mourn," producing the phrase "mourning 89.6.4." On the left side of the stamp, a red human figure blending into a red background that some deciphered as representing flowing blood. Ten thousand of these stamps were issued before the authorities suddenly banned their sale, and rumor had it that the stamp's designer was arrested. As a result, the stamps that had made it into pubic circulation and could not be recalled became valuable collector's items in China and among Chinese overseas.

A former student had secretly given me one of the stamps as a souvenir. I never guessed that this stamp would bring me such misfortune. There's a Chinese saying: The only crime of a common man is owning something precious. Greed, one of the great evils of mankind, is everywhere. I could only surmise that one of the Hong Kong immigration officials or police officers came up with the idea of taking personal possession of this valuable stamp, and therefore hid away all of my identity documents and then avoided further trouble by sending the three of us back to China without caring what would become of us.

I'm sure it never occurred to anyone at the Hong Kong Immigration Department that I would eventually make my way back to Hong Kong and demand my identity documents and postage stamp from them. But they categorically denied possessing my items, and claimed that I had signed an acknowledgement of receiving them back. They had hurriedly pressed me to sign that document just before we left, and I'd signed it without knowing its detailed content. I thought it was a document releasing me from that place, having not been told that we were being repatriated to the mainland.

The Hong Kong Immigration Department repatriated me to Guangdong once again without telling me where I was being sent. When I asked, "Where am I going?", a fat police officer gave me a wink and slyly replied, "We're sending you to America!" Once again I was loaded into a black van with dozens of other ordinary illegal immigrants and sent straight back to China. That satirical and insulting remark is something I'll never forget, and throughout my adversity it impelled me to never give up. A real man takes insult as a motivation.

My Second Imprisonment: Becoming Spartacus

The day I was repatriated, I was immediately arrested in Guangdong's Zengcheng County. It turned out that the public security bureau had already issued a warrant regarding my disappearance, and the minute I climbed out of the van at the Zengcheng custody center, the policemen there recognized me from the poster on the wall. I was once again escorted to the Guangzhou Municipal No. 1 Detention Center and locked up in the same cell as before. This time, the authorities didn't try me in open court, but summarily sentenced me to two years of "re-education through labor." Two months later, I was sent to the Guangzhou Municipal No. 1 Re-education Through Labor Center in Chini Town, on the distant outskirts of Guangzhou.

The heavy labor I was forced to engage in for long hours was an additional punishment. During the day I carried rocks at a wharf, and at night I made artificial flowers in the labor camp. Prisoners' workdays lasted more than fourteen hours, until deep into the night. Sometimes we were forced to rush an order, even working through the night. The prisoners were nothing more than money-making instruments for corrections system cadres.

Here I underwent a physiological change opposite to what I experienced in the detention center. Long hours of hard laboring in the sun turned my skin dark and tough; if my body suffered any kind of external trauma or injury, I recovered very easily. One time, my right leg became trapped between rocks that rolled down from the top of a pile. In that moment, I had the horrifying thought that I would lose my leg. Yet my leg was only bruised for a few days before miraculously recovering.

The prison cadres appointed trusties as overseers to closely monitoring the labor of more than 300 prisoners in penal servitude. The trusties, called team leaders, always blatantly boasted that they'd became team leaders because their family members pulled strings or paid off the prison cadres. That's why they were assigned the task of supervising other prisoners without having to do any hard work themselves.

At the wharf, with its turbid river water under a blazing sun, I witness scenes right out of the movie *Spartacus*. Abuse, violence and terror were the order of the day. The overseers would maltreat or beat prisoners for any reason, or no reason at all. Prisoners would be beaten for failing to satisfy the excessive production assignments; for pausing for a moment to catch their breath or get a drink of water; for the slightest complaint or even for a resentful facial expression.

Seven or eight trusties and prison cadres would gang up against a single prisoner, kicking him or beating him with clubs until he was covered with blood and couldn't even crawl to his feet. Sometimes the prisoner would lose consciousness, at which point he would have cold water dashed on him and then be beaten again.

Surrounded by malign forces, prisoners could only choke in silent fury. I detested this lawless place and the despots who took advantage of the situation to bully others. I set my mind to getting back at them once and for all.

Rising to fame with one battle

Because of my special status, I enjoyed a degree of respect in the eyes of guards and prisoners. Although I never fulfilled my "production assignments," most of the prison cadres were willing to turn a blind eye and not punish me for it. Even so, "The palace eunuch takes umbrage when the emperor does not," and some trusties vented their anger on me in order to impress prison officials.

One time at the artificial flower factory, a trusty used my failure to meet the production quota as a pretext for throwing his weight around, roughly twisting my left arm behind my back. As it happened, I had learned some self-defense skills and regularly practiced taichi, so I instinctively twisted sharply to the right, a move known as "The lion turns its head," and then gripped his neck with my right hand. This freed my left arm, while the force of my right hand sent the trusty tumbling to the floor.

Faster than words can tell, the other seven or eight trusties pounced like wolves and began kicking and punching me. As I fought for my life, my eyeglasses went flying through the air. Finally they pushed me onto a table and held down my hands and feet, asking if I surrendered. I thundered, "No!", my eyes flashing like lightning. Some prisoners began cheering for me. Afterwards I myself was amazed at how in an instant my usual feeling of terror was replaced with raw courage. I saw one of the trusties who was holding me down look hesitant, perhaps awed by my vehemence, and his raised fist wavered, stopping short of pounding me, and finally lowered.

It was psychological warfare, and I felt proud even in defeat. From a psychological standpoint, I had prevailed over that band of trusties. One of the prisoners had picked up my glasses for safekeeping, and as he gave them back to me afterwards, he furtively raised his thumb, his eyes full of admiration. With that one battle, I rose to fame. An increasing number of prisoners grouped around me, respecting not only my education but also my guts. Gradually I became a leader in their eyes, and imperceptibly they became my security screen. The trusties didn't dare pick on me from then on.

After that, I often held discussions about regulations and prison rules, and secretly wrote a letter to the provincial party committee and provincial government appealing to them to honor their own laws and stop the violence at the RTL camps. The provincial authorities responded, and after a word from them, the administrators of the RTL camp made a show of prohibiting brute management and implementing "civilized management." For a period of time, there was a significant reduction in violence at the RTL camp, and prisoners were allowed to catch their breath. (After I left, however, prisoners who came out after me said that the RTL center authorities quickly resumed brute management, and the violence was as bad as ever.)

A prison letter about blood-stained flowers

Gradually I came to notice that the labels stuck to the artificial flowers we produced had English-language trademarks and prices in U.S. dollars. I wondered if the flowers we made were being used for export. I knew that the laws of the United States and many other countries prohibited the import or export of products made by prisoners, because this was considered uncompensated slave labor. Keeping my eyes out, I learned from prison guards that these products were affiliated with a Hong Kong company. I surmised that the artificial flowers were re-exported through Hong Kong and were very likely sold in English-speaking countries such as the U.S.

I decided to expose this scandal, first in order to attack the CCP's reeducation through labor apparatus, and secondly to reduce the burden on prisoners. I was normally watched very carefully, not only by prison guards and trusties, but also by prisoners whom the prison authorities had instructed to pretend to be friendly with me. My only opportunity was in bed late at night, when I would take out pen and paper and write the letter bit by bit using the feeble streetlight that came through the window. At any sound or movement, I pretended to be asleep. This continued for several nights until I completed the letter.

Finally an opportunity presented itself. When a freighter came for a load of rocks, I found a moment when no one was looking and slipped my letter, along with 50 *yuan* that I kept on me (rolled up together and fastened with a rubber band), to one of the deck hands. He took the little bundle expressionlessly, as if nothing had happened, but gave a slight nod of his head. After the stones were loaded and the freighter blew its whistle and pulled away from the dock, I was finally able to relax.

This seemingly ordinary letter was addressed to three organizations: The UN Commission on Human Rights, Voice of America and Asia Human Rights Watch. Apart from my description of conditions in the RTL camp, the letter contained several original trademarks so the international community could investigate whether the artificial flowers we manufactured were being exported to foreign countries. My plan was for this letter to first be mailed to a friend in Guangzhou, who would then take it to Hong Kong, and a friend in Hong Kong would deliver it to the relevant international organizations.

While in the RTL camp, I was able to see an elder step-brother who worked in Guangzhou and sometimes came to visit me. Several months after I sent out the letter, there was still no reaction in the international community. Through my step-brother I learned that my friends or the international organizations didn't dare go public for fear of life-threatening retaliation against me in the RTL camp. I was angry and told my step-brother to tell my friends, "Whoever refuses to make this public is a traitor for the ages!"

I suddenly recalled the paragraph I wrote at the end of the letter: "I know very well that after this letter is published, I may be subjected to grave persecution and even more severe control, and could even lose my life. But I have no other choice!"

That helped me understand the hesitation and misgivings of those outside. I assured my step-brother, "Don't worry. I may be living in the tiger's mouth, but I'm as secure as Mount Tai." That saying from the Three Kingdoms period was what Zhuge Liang told his sovereign, Liu Bei, before he was sent as an envoy to the kingdom of Wu. What he meant was that he would rely on his own intelligence and resourcefulness while in dangerous territory and then retreat intact. My situation in the RTL center had gradually changed. The prison cadres avoided me, and many fellow prisoners had become my invisible security force, so I felt secure.

Finally the letter was published. A human rights organization found the artificial flowers I helped to make in a California shopping center; the product was identical, and the trademark and price in US dollars were the same. ABC Television, Voice of America and other major media produced special reports on the issue. The U.S.-based Laogai Research Foundation also published a special report entitled "Blood-stained Flowers." U.S. Customs took action and banned the import of these kinds of artificial flowers. The U.S. government made representations to the Chinese government that this was a case of slave labor being used for exports. The Chinese government was left speechless in the face of irrefutable evidence, because up until then, Beijing had categorically denied exporting goods produced by slave labor. The U.S. Congress or government at the same time demanded that the Chinese government unconditionally release me from custody.

After I arrived in the United States, I learned that I was the first person to send evidence to the international community of China exporting goods produced in prison. The letter I wrote and the trademarks included in it are now displayed in the Laogai Museum in Washington DC.

"You caused me to lose two million!" an RTL camp official wearing the insignia of "brigade head" yelled at me. He stared at me ferociously, roaring and circling around me. I kept silent, certain that he would not dare resort to violence against me. The RTL camp's artificial flower business had been temporarily suspended.

Pressure on the Chinese government from the international community, and unwillingness to continue accommodating "troublemakers" like me in RTL camps, resulted in my being released five months early. I regained my freedom in March 1995.

10. My Long Road to Exile, Far from Home

The authorities continued to tail me and keep me under surveillance, and occasionally called me in for questioning. Although no longer physically in prison, I remained imprisoned in spirit. Indeed, China had become one enormous prison for me. At that time a public security official intimated to me that if I wanted to leave China, a passport could be arranged. I said, "I'm already over thirty. I'm afraid I can't survive overseas." The public security official told me, "We're still uneasy about you. Democracy activists like you will either keep going to prison, or will have to leave the country."

Advised to leave China, I go into exile

During many conversations, Guangdong public security officials spoke in a way that revealed a thread of good intentions toward me personally. What they implied was, "Leave! You need to get out of here! You can't win against this government, so why sacrifice yourself for nothing?" In Guangzhou I heard this kind of thing from people connected with the government: "Back in 1989, the Guangdong government delayed arresting you for two months after the June 4th massacre in Beijing as a hint that you should flee the country. They gave you time, but you didn't leave!"

There's no way to confirm whether this was the case. In fact, after the Tiananmen massacre, the Communist authorities used two main methods against dissidents: imprisonment or exile, both of which cut off contact between dissidents and the general public. This is how the Communists monopolized power and vigorously defended their vested interests. As the Song dynasty historian Li Tao wrote, "How can an outsider be allowed to sleep alongside one's bed?" In the twenty-first century, the minds of the rulers in Beijing are still suffused with the past teachings of China's ancient feudal rulers.

Considering how remaining in China under tight surveillance would make it difficult for me to achieve anything, I felt it might be better to leave for a while and see the world. Consequently, with the help of Asia Human Rights Watch and with an invitation from Columbia University in New York, I went into exile as a visiting scholar, setting off for the United States in the winter of 1996. While passing through Hong

Kong, I recalled the insulting remarks of the fat Hong Kong police officer and sighed: I'm like Song Jiang or Liu Bei in ancient times, suffering countless misfortunes and humiliations, but finally escaping the sea of terror. As I bade farewell to China in the biting cold wind, I couldn't hold back my tears. Ironically, Hong Kong, which had denied me entry years ago, became the only tiny patch of Chinese soil that I could visit during my life in exile, even though it was nothing like China.

Not long after that, in 1997, Hong Kong returned to Chinese sovereignty. I continued to visit Hong Kong several more times, but stopped after the cross-border kidnapping of several publishers and booksellers by the Chinese authorities in 2015. More recently, I have visited Taiwan almost every year, taking it as my second homeland because of its genuine traditional Chinese culture and modern democratic politics. I understand Taiwanese people's insistence on firmly defending their independence and dignity.

The heavy door of China closed behind me, and my long road of exile began. Passing from China to the outside world, I experienced the "besieged city effect" – while inside I wanted to leave, but when outside I wanted to go back inside. Homesickness and nostalgia plagued me with insomnia. My dreams were filled with scenes from my youth in my home village in northern Sichuan, among the precipitous mountains where rivulets thundered during the rainy season. Truly, as the Southern Tang ruler Li Yu once wrote, "Bathed in bright moonlight, the old country is overwhelming."

From student to principal: An American story

Settling in New York, I found it hard to survive at first. Fortunately I could tolerate hardship, and I worked ceaselessly at any job I could find, regardless of wages or prestige, including shop salesman, data processer, gardener and tour guide. My income was meagre, and I was always pressed for money. I consoled myself that it was still better than China, because I was a free agent and didn't have to put up with surveillance and persecution.

After two years, I decided to take a computer course, hoping it would help me find a stable job. The computer industry was fiercely competitive at that time. I signed up for a computer training school run by Chinese owners in the heart of Manhattan. What I learned was that I had less aptitude for operating computers than other people. At the same time, I noticed that business at the computer school was not good. As I came to know the proprietors, I casually gave them suggestions such as creating ads to attract students, as well as ways to improve the school's management.

In China I had studied management and taught economics, and during my spells of freedom after my two terms of imprisonment, I'd held positions as manager of a foreign enterprise and deputy general manager of a private firm. The poor management of the computer school disturbed me.

"What would you think if I hired you as general manager of the school?" one of the computer school proprietors asked me one day out of the blue. I was startled; after all, I was there as a student. But considering my ineptitude with computers, I couldn't help mulling over the idea that I might be better suited for management.

Why not give it a try? With this mindset, after thinking it over for a few days, I accepted the proprietor's offer. My first move as general manager was to shift the school's target market from Chinese immigrants to local American residents in general, and to put greater effort into attracting native English speakers. At the same time, I expanded the course offerings to give students more options and better equip them for the local employment market. After a month working from dawn to dusk and hardly remembering to eat, I turned the money-losing computer school around, and it began to show a profit.

From then on, profits increased or remained stable month to month. As the computer school gradually expanded, my status also changed from a salaried general manager to a school director with management shares. Later, when the company was reorganized, I became one of the proprietors with an actual shareholding. When New York was struck by the 9-11 terrorist attacks in 2001, students were unwilling to take courses in Manhattan and shifted to the outer boroughs, nearly causing the computer school to fold. Yet, with willpower and savvy, I pulled the school through what turned out to be just one of many crises. Over the years, I led the school calmly and adapted to changing circumstances, keeping the school from closing during one market crisis after another.

The school constantly changed its business model. Courses were expanded from the computer field to accounting, medical billing and other fields, and the language domain was also expanded to accommodate not only local residents but also international students. Finally it was forged into an international school in the heart of Manhattan. The number of students increased from fewer than twenty to more than a hundred, and then to several hundred.

While engaged in the Herculean task of running a school, I was also studying at Columbia University. I worked diligently night and day and passed through one round after another of examinations and dissertation defenses. Like full-time students, I managed to complete my studies and receive my Master's degree in public administration within two years.

Those around me hailed my experience from student to principal as a classic American success story. In this great land of freedom, full of challenges and opportunities, I accepted the challenges and took advantage of the opportunities. I was fortunate enough to achieve and bear witness to what people call the American Dream.

Apart from taking the approach of "the early bird catches the worm," working untiringly and enduring hardship, and quickly-wittedly adapting to change, I attribute my success to a "secret" that is not really secret: I observe the strong points of Americans and their standards of behavior, reflect on the shortcomings of Chinese and the vicious circles in their thinking, and constantly adjust and raise myself to a higher level. I've noticed that some Chinese fail in America because they continue to employ the opportunistic philosophy of the Chinese in the civilized world. Taking this as a warning, I regularly review my own actions, striving to squeeze out all remnants of the inveterate bad traits of the Chinese and the wolf genes of the Communist Party, and to thoroughly reform and remold myself. Abiding by the open and aboveboard dealings of the civilized world, I've abandoned dishonest practices common among the Chinese in what I consider an even more meaningful application of the saying, "When in Rome, do as the Romans do."

A worldwide following in the media and on the internet

Apart from my activities in the commercial sphere, I have not abandoned the democratic cause. While in exile, I have diligently continued writing, frequently publishing political commentaries and books in an effort to inspire and influence my fellow Chinese. I've published a series of books in Hong Kong, Taiwan and Japan, several of which have been best-sellers. They include *Machiavelli in Beijing*, *If the US and China Go to War*, *100 Basic Facts about China* and *The Unwelcome Chinese*.

My years of experience, habit of contemplation and skill at self-expression have gradually made me into one of the most frequent political commentators on several overseas Chinese-language television and radio programs. Voice of America, Radio Free Asia, New Tang Dynasty Television, Sanlih E-Television of Taiwan, KAZN 1300 AM in Los Angeles... my voice and image are all over the high-frequency airwaves.

Sometimes when I go to Chinese neighborhoods, people recognize me and come over to shake my hand, eagerly telling me about their sorrow over China's corruption and their yearning for a democratic China. My readers, radio and television audiences and internet followers can be found all over the world, including inside China. I often receive email from people in China giving me information that is sealed off within China, or expressing their respect. I'm moved by the support and encouragement of these awakened Chinese, which has become the greatest impetus for me to continue the struggle. The road is long, but I am ever mindful of my brainwashed and persecuted countrymen, our national image despoiled by Communist autocracy, and the radiance of democratic ideals. My struggle has not ended, and I am determined to change all of this.

With the rapid expansion of the internet, in 2017 I began producing a YouTube program to disseminate universal values. Drawing on analysis of the current political situation, I educate Chinese all over the world about democracy, along with political analysis. Chinese inside and outside of China eagerly jumped aboard, and my YouTube channel rapidly attracted a large and lively following that made me one of the most famous and popular overseas Chinese YouTubers. I've felt obliged to upload a video every day to ensure that I don't disappoint the support and expectations of my followers. It has become a part of my daily work that I don't interrupt even on holidays and weekends.

Starting in August 2018, something unusual developed on my YouTube channel; the number of subscribers not only stopped growing, but also took an unusual downward turn month by month. YouTube didn't reply to my inquiries and offered little explanation for this strange phenomenon.

After spending some time gaining an understanding from various parties, I've reached a general conclusion: Many China-based netizens have to surmount the Chinese government's Great Firewall in order to view or subscribe to my YouTube channel, so Chinese State Security departments made use of this to create fake group subscriptions and then cancel them, misleading the YouTube management into believing there are fake subscriptions and therefore canceling them. This has led to normal subscriptions also being canceled.

Other possibilities include: Red spies working behind the scenes in companies such as Google or YouTube to target Chinese-language channels that propagate universal values, and employing covert manipulation to cancel subscriptions, as Chinese telecommunications giant Huawei has been doing; Direct espionage and internet attacks, for example Chinese State Security departments directly launching internet attacks from Chinese soil to obstruct or cancel the subscriptions of Chinese netizens; or pro-CCP outsourcing Mandarin- Language companies deceiving YouTube or Google.

(After several time reporting to FBI, situation was changed from March of 2019. This part needs to be updated.)

In spite of encountering such difficulties, I persist in producing my videos every day, because I know that netizens who hope and struggle for China's democratization look forward to my daily interpretations of the current situation. Although the number of subscribers has decreased, my viewership numbers remain stable between 100,000 and 200,000, or sometimes even more.

On June 1, 2017, I was invited to take part in the Oxford Union debate, delivering a speech entitled "While China's Overseas Impact is Growing, Its Role is Destructive Rather Than Constructive." On May 3, 2018, I was invited to take part in the Cambridge Union debate and delivered a speech entitled "If China is Not Democratized, The Future Will Not Belong to The East." Both speeches were very well received. These debates and speeches opened a new English-language world. Chinese inside and outside of China have always encouraged me to enter the English-language world in order to disseminate my thinking and viewpoints to the entire world, to be a champion of justice for the Chinese people enslaved by the Communist system, and to add a true Chinese voice to the uproar over "China's rise."

Traversing the world but unable to enter my native land

While in Geneva for the Tibet-China Conference in 2009, some other participants and I made a pilgrimage to the former home of the philosopher Jean-Jacques Rousseau. The small, simple home on the second floor of a building in Geneva's old city revealed the living conditions in exile of this pioneer of human rights. Browsing through eighteenth-century paintings of people and scenery while listening to a narration through my earphones, I imagined Rousseau's peripatetic life and sighed at how this kind of exile disappeared in the West long ago, but has yet to end in twenty-first century China. This shows that China needs at least 200 years to catch up with the West!

"Do not return home before you have passed your prime of life; it must break your heart," wrote the Tang poet Wei Zhuang. While I was in prison, I added the sentence, "Do not return home when you are old, either, for it will absolutely break your heart." These lines of poetry seem more applicable than ever to my life today, as time passes like a river or like electricity.

I've visited nearby Asian countries many times, but I'm unable to enter the gate of China. Only my own country denies me admittance. Watching China's direction from afar with glistening eyes, my heart is as heavy as a stone. Whenever my flight takes off from Asia for North America, I silently pray for family members and old friends, my countrymen and my homeland. When will the clouds part to offer a glimpse of blue sky? As I fly ever further across the Pacific, I am full of homesickness and longing for my native land.

Made in the USA
Columbia, SC
22 August 2022